The West and its people,

Like cactus and bobwire,

May be sharp and prickly,

Or rusted and sickly,

But they sure have their good points.

Runaway Cowboy©

Skip-Don Publications®

First Edition, 160 pages, illustrated

Library of Congress Catalogue Card Number. 96-93114

ISBN No. 0-9656523-0-0 (Pbk.)

Printed 1997 in the United States of America

by

Ben-Wal Printing
Pomona, California

Skip-Don Publications

117 White Chapel Drive
Benicia, CA 94510
and
6420 Euston Drive
Amarillo, TX 79109

RUNAWAY COWBOY

by

Edwin L. Skipworth
of
Amarillo, Texas

(The Panhandle's sagebrush philosopher)

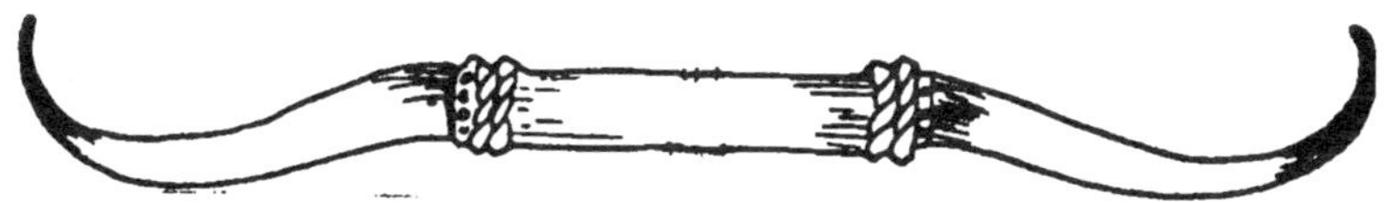

as told to

Don Keller
of
Benicia, California

1996

CONTENTS

Episodes:

ACKNOWLEDGMENTS

The author and editor wish to thank A.W. Erwin, the great cowboy cartoonist who has published many of his own books of cartoon jokes. In typical cowboy friendliness, he donated his artwork to illustrate this book, and we are deeply indebted to him.

We also wish to thank the publishers of McCormack's Guides of California,, Allen Kanda and Don McCormack. Don's technical advice on publishing and distribution was of immeasurable help. Allen continuously helped coax the editor's computer into the intricate maneuvers that the editor was unable to accomplish by himself.

Leonard Pressley Ashton, the author's brother-in-law, made the book complete with his companion story of his own experience of running away as a youth in cowboy country.

Finally, gratitude is not nearly a strong enough word for Wilsie Ashton Skipworth, Skip's wife. Helping every step of the way, offering not only advice but constant support, she has proven to be the linchpin of love that made it possible.

#

The bunkhouse waddie with the longest reach
always gets the most to eat.

PREFACE

The author, a resident of Amarillo, Texas,
has very long arms.
He lived the cowboy's rugged life.
He deserves the biggest steak.

* * *

Don Keller served primarily as editorial watchdog, making corrections, proofreading for spelling, grammar, punctuation, libel, continuity, and performing the desk-top publishing chores of page makeup, inserting the cartoons and other artwork, coordinating with the publisher and artist.

Don is a semi-retired journalist, having worked for metropolitan daily newspapers both in Southern California and the San Francisco Bay Area. He was a reporter, columnist, city editor and managing editor for more than 40 years. Until recently, he also served as a firearms safety and marksmanship instructor and rifle range officer for YMCA Camp Dudley, the oldest summer camp for boys in the nation, at Westport in upstate New York's beautiful Adirondack Mountains along Lake Champlain.

* * *

The editor, a resident of Benicia, California,
has short arms.
He lived a city slicker's life.
He deserves the smallest steak.

These pages are dedicated

To my lovely wife, Wilsie, my little Princess and best friend, whose love, encouragement and inspiration kept me focused on these stories;

To my newspaperman friend for many years, Don Keller, who saw a book in these stories and whose brilliant editing and gentle prodding made it happen;

And
To A.W. Erwin, whose wonderful "Cowtoons" so aptly and humorously illustrate the frustrations and foibles of everyday cowboy life.

Skip

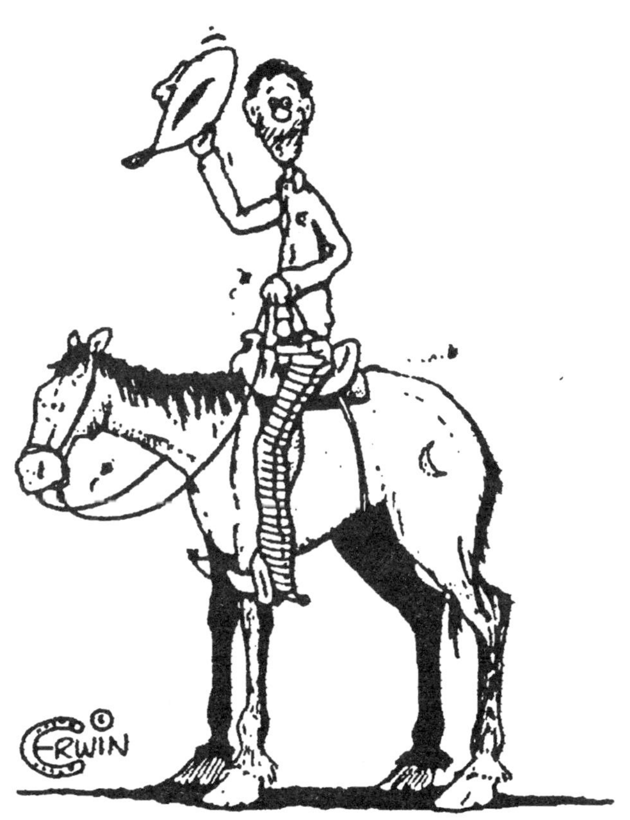

INTRODUCTION

My early memories of Skip, when I was newly married and a cub reporter for a Southern California daily newspaper, have absolutely nothing to do with cowboy stories.

The memories? A gift-wrapped box full of wood ashes sitting on the porch of my in-laws on Christmas morning. A note attached said the ashes were a clue as to what would be arriving soon—a cord of wood, the most practical gift of all, one that would be enjoyed night after night in front of a crackling blaze in the fireplace.

The memories also are of an album full of commercial-quality color photographs of dolls that had been custom-made by Dolly, my wonderful mother-in-law. They were another unusual gift from "Skip" Skipworth, a photography buff helping Dolly to sell her exquisite dolls.

Those are the types of things that typify this most unusual man. Of his personal life in California we knew only that he worked at Lockheed Aircraft Corp. in Burbank, California, and lived in San Fernando Valley.

Regarding his Texas connection, we knew only that he was a native of Texas. "Native" turned out to be a gross understatement. We didn't learn until more than 40 years later how his formative years had been spent on the plains of the Texas Panhandle, doing all the mysterious and onerous chores that have managed to work their way into the legends of America's Odyssey, the Old West.

To those who worked on the western ranches, those days offered nothing more than day-to-day chores, hot, bone-tiring, back-aching drudgery that had to be done if one were to survive. And if one were to just get enough grub money together to keep a little meat on the bones and to have a bedroll or bunkhouse to collapse into at the end of each long, frying, sun-baked day or wind-whipped freezing night.

To those of us who have never had the experience, perhaps even the honor, of having lived the life of a legend, Skip's tales sometimes sound like he looks, too tall to be true. But every word is a factual testament to the life of the cowboy during the depression years. They were as hard, sometimes as exciting, and occasionally as frightening, as those of the pioneers who earlier had headed west to start a new type of life in frontier America.

But Skip never talked about those days. How we learned of his cowboy days with its alien lifestyle—alien to us, anyway—came about in an unusual way. He acquired a manual typewriter with large type so he could write to his wife's sister-in-law, who was losing her eyesight, in Texas. There were many other relatives with whom Skip wanted to keep up correspondence.

So he put some of those missives into a newsletter format, cranked duplicates out on a copying machine and began mailing them. They
went to relatives and to the dozens of other friends who had been drawn to him over the years by his friendly, helpful, shy and totally unassuming demeanor.

He whimsically dubbed his growing group of friends, "The Cactus Club." And his newsletter, which he published with surprising frequency—sometimes weekly—was called the "Godzilla Report." He named the newsletter, Godzilla, after that cranky old manual typewriter, on which he began his communication efforts before graduating into massaging a computer.

Many of the entries in the Godzilla Report were—and still are—stories submitted by his legion of friends from many states throughout the west. Some are nothing more than letters his myriad admirers sent to him. He urged friends to offer submissions. He turned nothing down. He praised all for their efforts. And always thanked them profusely.

He mailed copies to dozens

of friends on his growing mailing list. He compiled another list, of birthdays and anniversaries. Everyone got remembered, sometimes with a notation in the Godzilla Report, sometimes with a beautifully hand-drawn card. His postage bills mounted, but he kept on, week after week, month after month.

One day, many months after he began his interstate homilies with a rapidly expanding army of readers, he wrote of an episode (first chapter of this book) from his family history. Friends asked for more. Thus began an almost weekly continuum of the Skipworth Saga, his Depression Years of being "Home on the Range." He made the physically demanding, excruciatingly difficult work sound like fun. It was his straightforward writing style, his softness of chosen word, that made it all so appealing.

I sent an e-mail message to him, suggesting it was of book quality. He demurred, doubting it. We insisted in another e-mail message. Do you really think so, he asked incredulously. Yes, yes, yes. We persisted.

Soon afterward, his stepdaughter, Donna Steger, telephoned him on his 80th birthday. Dad, she said, this is good enough to be published. That must have convinced him, and Skip and I began a lengthy and almost daily e-mail correspondence. "True Tales of a Tall Texan" is the result.

We hope you find a big, overstuffed chair to sit in while you peruse this very easy-to-read book. We hope you find it as much fun to read as all the "zillion members of The International Cactus Club" have found it to be.

What you are about to read is told straight-forward, no frills, no fancy language...just the way it happened, pardner.

—— Don Keller

FORWARD

This book was written entirely via e-mail. From its inception, all communication between Edwin "Skip" Skipworth and Don Keller was done on their computers. The e-mail letters continued almost daily for many, many months. They took on a life of their own, each generating puns, more humorous anecdotes and cowboy lingo as the product came together.

Skip was asked for a brief biography to be inserted in the book. He replied, "How about if I put down everything I can think of and you sift out the chaff and boil it down to the consistency of cowboy coffee?"

Because place names would be mentioned in the book, an explanation of geographical terminology might be needed. So research was done on the area. In writing to Skip about the Texas Panhandle, Don wrote:

"The High Plains, also known as the Staked Plains or Llano Estacado, includes all but the easternmost fringe of the 175-mile-wide by 375-mile-long Texas Panhandle, whose area is approximately 45,000 square miles. The surface is almost flat and represents one of the largest tracts of uninterrupted level land in the world.

"Only two permanent rivers run through it, the Canadian, through a canyon called the 'Breaks,' and the Pecos, which runs through a wide valley called the Toyah Basin."

Skip's e-mail reply:

"However did you find out what the term 'staked plains' actually means? If you don't really know, your research is incomplete. It is tacitly understood that the early Italian explorer, Colombo, wired his report to the Duke of Marlboro, saying, 'Jeeze! Its so gol-derned windy here that if you don't stake things down they blow into the next county.' I can vouch for his accuracy."

Don asked Skip for the definitions of several words relating to tackle used by cowboys.

Skip's reply:

"Snaffle"...What happens to your nose when you've been out in blowing dirt too long.

"Latigo"...What you have after waking up from a night on the town.

"Pommel"...Its the part of the saddle you beat on when you've lost your rope.

"Remuda"...A group of Mexican horses, or Texas jassonkeys.

"Cantle"...That's the part you beat on if you're left-handed.

Surcingle"...That's a rope or strap around the beast's chest that litte kids whose pappa can't afford a saddle hang on to. Also rodeo bull riders.

"Hackamore"...Its a bitless bridle made of rope or leather that permits your horse to graze at night while you're in a sleeping bag with assorted rattlesnakes. You tie a rope to the Hackamore and stake the other end to the high plains.

That's the way it went, day after day. Part of the routine was for Skip and Don to address each other with a new nickname each time, signing off with a new handle of his own. In turn, the other made up still another name for his counterpart, also signing off with a different name, the salutations and replies often relating to each other and to the day's subject.

Some of the more memorable monikers were Texas Fats, Bovine Battler, Patience, Godzilla, Texas Rangy, The Lone Stranger, Greenhorn, Ripehorn, Tall Fat Texan, The Vicarious Wrangler, Too Tall Texan, Whiffy Lee, Saddle Sore, Hogleg, Downwind Dude, Bull Thrower, Great Donzilla, Panhandle Princess and the Frog, Square Shooter, Slick (as calf slobber), Hogleg, Cow Patty, Bull Durham, Slick (as a greased saddle rope), Bull, Bob Wire, Bull Oney, Bull Etin, Cow Poke, Bull Emia, Whip Persnapper, Whip Pingboy, Swanky Lanky, Hanky Panky, Whip Lash, Bull Headed, Henny Penny, Al Tercation, Pecos Kid, Benicia Bob Cat, High Pockets, Lightning Rod, Thunder Mug.

When asked about cowboy lingo that he and the other

"waddies" used on the range, Skip forwarded such as the following glossary:

Dogie: A calf that's lost its mammy and whose pappy and is running around with other cows.

Ugly as home-made sin: Describing a situation; or another cowboy's girlfriend or wife, but not in his presence.

Waddies, wranglers, drifters (self-description): Denoting lack of permanent attachment to a regular job.

"I been uh aimin' to think about a-doin' that": Refers, of course, to habitual putter-offers.

In the beginning, the two talked about a pen name for Skip. When they lived in Southern California for many years, Don and all his relatives had known Skip as Buster, to which—in his self-effacing manner—he never objected. But when it was suggested he be named on the title

page, "Big Buster Skipworth," his reply, as usual, was straightforward.

"When the time came I was going to ask for your thoughts on a title, but now I'm not so sure. "Big Buster' in this end of these United States would be tantamount, or worse, to naming me, "Big Bubba," and you can't get that much more worser than that (Country talk, Tex/ Mex)."

Skip later explained that "Buster" was a common baby name, that he hoped he had outgrown it by his 80th birthday. And that is exactly how old he was before his California friends became enlightened and began calling him Skip.

#

ABOUT THE ARTIST

All artwork in this book is from the pen of A.W. Erwin of Graham, Texas. His HOOVES & HORNS "cowtoons" appear in newspapers, magazines, newsletters, the calendars and greeting cards he produces and markets. Not wanting to detract from his down-home humor in all of his art, we have chosen not to include the captions associated with each. We have used only those "cowtoons" which we found help tell the story line in this book. Throughout, you also will see small "signature" cartoons. They are excised portions of other "cowtoons" and are also from his talented pen.

A.W. Erwin was born in Cowtown (Fort Worth), during the late 50s and was raised near the farm and ranch community of Jean, Texas. The family raised cattle, a few horses and most anything else they needed.

From a very early age he displayed a unique talent for drawing, with a brand of humor all his own. When A.W. wasn't busy on the homestead he hired out to local outfits to work cattle, build fences, haul hay or help out during harvest. FFA, Vocational Ag. and too many bulls and broncs finished out his high school years in nearby Graham, where he still resides with Pam, the high school sweetheart he married soon after graduation, and their two sons, Aaron and Frankie.

The next several years he spent building cattle pens, barns and more fences. Eventually he settled down to drawing his cowtoons. We're mighty glad he did.

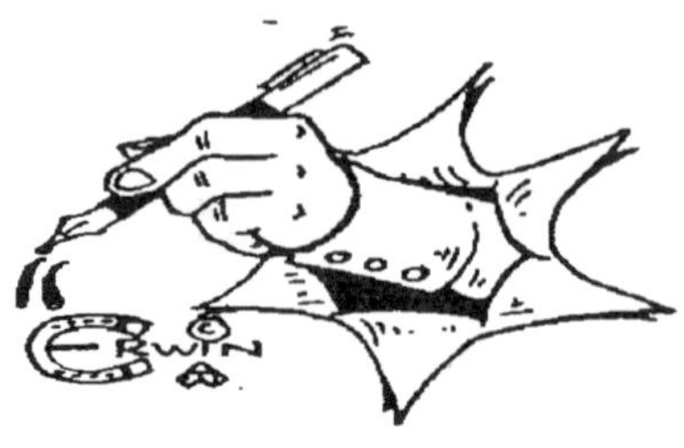

PROLOGUE

The great Ben Franklin once penned these lines—"If you would not be forgotten as soon as you are dead, either write things worth remembering or do things worth writing."

Octogenarian Edwin "Skip"Skipworth did both. He lived these memorable true adventures of ranching and cowboys during the Great Depression. That period of strange and difficult times is interwoven throughout this book.

Several years after those not-so-halcyon cowboy days, he met his first wife, Vivian, in Lubbock, Texas. It was a love-at-first-sight romance leading to their marriage. Two years later they moved to Los Angeles.

After three years of temporary and part-time work, Skip was employed by Lockheed and remained there until early retirement some 35 years later. In the early '40s, Vivian and Skip were living in Glendale, where Don Keller met Skip and they became lifelong friends. During the later years, Vivian's health, already marginal, started failing. She died in 1982.

Subsequently, Vivian's niece, a really cute little girl named Wilsie Steger, lost her husband, Luther. After not having even seen each other for more than 40 years, Wilsie and Skip met again. It was love at first sight all over again. They were wed in 1990 and are happily married. Wilsie has five adult children and is 15 years Skip's junior—a rather happy arrangement.

Wilsie—she also was born and raised in the Texas Panhandle—and Skip could no longer resist the urge of living among people of sod and saddle. In 1992, they moved back to the Panhandle and live in Amarillo.

#

EPISODE ONE

He got cleaned down to his spurs,
but a jury gave him fresh duds.

The Poker Game

This is the first of many true stories of the Old West. I saw this one in our town newspaper. It's full of intrigue, danger, daring and adventure. Date-lined Santa Fe (AP), it's a tale of historical importance (and some personal implications) because of a fairly recent, local hot political issue dealing with reservation casinos. Now to pick up the story from the newspaper:

> Who needs 'Gunsmoke?' Anyone hankerin' for good yarns about the Old West can simply go to the local law library and look up court rulings on an 1850s New Mexico gambling law—the same law invoked in a modern-day legal attack on Indian Casinos.
>
> Cases under the law date back to 1876 and involve tales of drunken gamblers, lots of saloons, thousands of dollars of cattle profits lost at the poker table and alleged horse-race cheats.
>
> Albuquerque lawyer Victor Marshall cited the territorial-era gambling law and some of the old court cases early this month when he filed a lawsuit against several banks and financial institutions that provide automatic teller machines and other services for Indian casinos.
>
> Marshall's clients are seeking to recover money lost wagering at casinos. The statute, listed in state law books dating from 1856-57, says any person losing at cards or a gambling device—or that person's relatives or heirs—can sue to recover money or property lost to gambling.

What follows is the Skipworth connection, one that will reappear repeatedly throughout this book:

> For sheer entertainment value, perhaps the best case to reach the state Supreme Court under the law was Snure vs. Skipworth, which the court decided in 1956.
>
> Ben P. Snure, described in the ruling as 'a young cattleman' from Arizona, showed up in Clovis in December 1954 with four

truckloads of cattle. He sold the livestock for $8,183, then headed for the Cattlemen's Club. Snure had been drinking and told the club's proprietor, Jack Skipworth, he wanted to get into a poker game.

Skipworth obliged (this was about midnight on Dec. 3) by calling a couple of players in Hobbs, 110 miles away. They arrived about 2 a.m. According to the court ruling, the poker game 'started at once, following receipt of a new deck of cards sent for by plaintiff (Snure) who seemed reluctant to play with any cards on the premises.' Despite this precaution, Snure didn't do well.

The game continued for 14 hours, with only a few interruptions, including one for Snure to obtain a $2,000 draft from his Arizona account to stay in the game. When the poker session finally broke up the afternoon of Dec. 4 Snure testified he'd lost $10,183.

Snure later sued the Hobbs men and Skipworth under the gambling recovery law. A jury found in his favor, and the Supreme Court affirmed the decision.

The Supreme Court noted that while Skipworth and the two Hobbs men never admitted to being professional gamblers, it was 'more than passing strange' Skipworth called poker men from Hobbs instead of rounding up some Clovis card players. And on a point of law, the court said it didn't matter that Snure actively sought the poker game—he still could sue to recover his losses.

* * * * * *

(Which just may go to prove you should never gamble with a man who knows both sides of the cards.)

The article, which appeared in the Amarillo Sunday News—Globe of Jan. 21, 1996, went on to describe some dozen other suits filed over the years, all interesting, some successful and some not, but it's the Skipworth connection I'd like to explore a little further.

I knew Jack. We rode and cowboyed together in New Mexico during part of my misspent youth. I haven't seen him since.

#

EPISODE TWO

In every boy there's a man,
In every man there's a boy.

The Great Depression

The small community of Kress in the Texas Panhandle is where I was born (in 1916) and raised. My family owned and operated a small farm, slightly more than 100 acres in cultivation, we had cows for milk and butter, horses to till the soil, chickens, a large garden area, a vineyard and fruit orchard. It was one of many farms sharing almost limitless prairie with large cattle ranches.

There were town socials and picnics, medicine shows, rodeos and all-day singing, even chautauquas and itinerant patriotic speakers, all tending to enhance community purpose and spirit. By today's standards, life was primitive, could be quite rugged and sometimes was cruel. But it was also good. Honesty, courtesy, decency, friendliness and helpfulness were words we all lived by.

Life for the Skipworth family was slightly better than most. The farm was paid for, free and clear; we were beholden to no man. And it was from this early period in my youth that I formed a lifelong affection and respect for the outgoing and down-to-earth people of sod and saddle.

In 1929, shortly after my 13th birthday, the world of finance crashed. So did my own family's world. In short succession, my father died, Wall Street plunged into the Great Depression, the bank collapsed with our savings, my father's life insurance company defaulted, prices for farm and ranch products hit rock bottom and a drought began which eventually resulted in the great Dust Bowl era. Without banks there was no money in circulation, and without money there was little commerce and few jobs.

My older brother, Willis, and sister, Bobbie Lee, were away at college. Our mother, Lucy, was uneasy about operating a farm under those conditions with only a 13-year-old boy. She accepted an invitation from relatives in Hattiesburg, Mississippi, for both of us to come stay with them until Mom decided what she wanted to do. She rented out the farm and house for the crop season and we left.

The Mississippi experience didn't work. Soon we moved to Littlefield, Texas, working and living on a commercial dairy with Lucy's stepdaughter and my half-sister, Mae Cundiff, and her family. Among others working and living at the dairy was a young man from Fort Sumner, New Mexico. His name was Richard Herring, and he was working his way through high school. He and I became good friends. I graduated from grade school that year and shortly thereafter Mom and I moved back to the farm.

We had a rude shock. The orchard was dead. So was the vineyard from lack of water, even though there were two working windmills. The chickens were gone. The chicken house had been dismantled and burned for firewood. Only 20 of the 100+ acres had been planted. That was in feed, but it hadn't been harvested. The stock were grazing it. Some of the fences were down with lengths of wire missing. A house window had been broken out and let the weather in. Hand tools were gone, as were some farm implements and furniture. It was not a happy homecoming.

I went to work on the outside and Mom on the inside. I gathered what I could of the feed crop and brought it in before it could be further trampled. I hooked up the horses and uprooted the dead fruit trees, chopped and stacked them for firewood, and set about making repairs to fences and equipment.

Mom scraped and scoured the inside of the house, put up fresh curtains and made it livable. She also borrowed a kerosene-fired incubator from a neighbor, bought several dozen fertile chicken eggs and set them to hatch to provide eggs and meat that winter. After I finished plowing the fields I got them ready to plant.

In those days, the accepted rule of familial responsibility in rural Texas was for the woman of the house to take care of the family, the house, garden, poultry and such, in addition to setting disciplinary and moral standards for the household to abide by. The man of the house helped his wife with the heavy stuff, maintained the home and buildings, took care of the animals and equipment and did the farming. It worked pretty well—most of the time.

It was at this point my mother and I began getting a little cross-wise with each other. As the only male at home, I saw myself as "the man of the house," with all the inherent duties and responsibilities, while my mother still saw me as a 13-year-old kid. Neither of us was willing to compromise, but in the end, it was she who was the Mom and made the Mom decisions.

Meanwhile, a new high school agriculture teacher moved to town. Fresh from an agriculture university, with degrees and teaching credentials and having been raised on a large farm and ranch himself, he decided to help me make a showplace of that small farm. We walked the acres together, made paper layouts and planned scientific farming methods such as contour-terracing to conserve rain water, crop-rotation to put nutrients back into the soil and even supplementing the cows' food to increase butter fat and milk yield. All standard procedures today.

Mom would listen patiently to each idea, and often looked convinced, but she'd always discuss it with neighboring farmers to get their advice. When they'd say—and they usually did—"Well, Aunt Lucy, I never heard of doing it that way; I think I'd be a might leery if I was you," that idea would be vetoed. Another Mom decision.

Lucy cannot be faulted. She was accepting the best advice of friends and neighbors, and the farm and kid were her responsibility. But it took the heart right out of the kid. Consequently, I finally decided to make a mid-puberty career decision. And that is why I ran away from home. It's too bad I couldn't see Lucy's point of view. In later years she referred to that period of our lives as "having walked up Fool's Hill together."

#

EPISODE THREE

The Lord pulled the cork enough
to bog a buzzard's shadow.

Runnin' Away

It was 1930 , I was 14 years old and typical of most of my run-aways, I headed west. It just always seemed the directional preference. I wanted to reach my cousins, Crutch Skipworth and his younger brother, Roy, who with their families had neighboring ranches somewhere near Fort Sumner. (I soon found out that "neighboring" meant about 15 to 20 miles in New Mexico.)

I had one ace in the hole, a friend in Fort Sumner named Richard Herring, whom I'd worked with on a dairy in Littlefield, Texas. The dairy belonged to the parents of Kathleen Cundiff Sheldon, my half-niece.

Richard's home was in Fort Sumner but he lived with and worked for the Cundiffs in Littlefield in order to attend high school there. Richard was working at a grocery store and surely would know of Crutch and Roy, which he did.

Jack Skipworth was Crutch's son, 2 or 3 years older than I and the only one of their children still at home. He was a riding, roping fool, and he and his dad would do anything in the world to test the mettle of a "tenderfoot" from Texas. I'll be telling you later about a wild horse ride those idiots suckered me into.

But let's fast-backward for a minute. Crutch and Roy were two of some 14 or so children of Uncle Finus Skipworth (whose mother was an Indian) and his wife. They were born in Kress, which was mostly built and populated by Skipworths. Uncle Finus, half-brother of Skip's father (but considerably older), was land-rich and, as his children married, gave each one a section of land as a wedding gift.

You may be wondering about that unusual name, Crutch. Later you'll read about Tom, a fellow I worked with briefly. But there was another Tom. He was the brother of Crutch and Roy. This Tom had several kids. He named one of them "Crutch" after his brother.

They called them "Big Crutch" and "Little Crutch" All my life I've tried to satisfy my curiosity as to how come that name of Crutch. I even asked Big Crutch, Finus' older son.

He laughed and said, "My pappa did it..." His pappa died when I was an infant. I never did find out why a fellow who was not lame was called Crutch.

When Crutch and Roy took wives, they soon traded their land for ranch land in New Mexico. As a child I remembered them mainly from their visits for occasional deaths or marriages in the family. Sometimes they'd bring little Jack and we'd play together.

I deeply admired their boots and big hats.

I left Kress for the Big Adventure mid-afternoon of a hot sultry day. I was wearing an old wide-brimmed hat, so floppy I had to safety-pin the front to the crown to keep it from flapping in my face, my best shoes (lace oxfords) and best shirt and pants. My other pants and shirt with changes of socks and underwear were packed in my trumpet case with my trumpet.

Also in the case was my most important asset, a birthday gift from Bobbie Lee, my sister. Seven years older than I, she was living and teaching in Dumas, Texas, during this period, except for summer vacations. What she had given me was a bag of 200 pennies she had saved. It was all the money I had.

A kid in my circumstances had two options for major travel then, either hitch-hike or ride the rods. I chose the first, and ultimately learned there's a lot more hiking than there is hitching.

I also very quickly learned that 200 pennies add a lot of weight to a trumpet case, but like American Express, I couldn't leave home without them. I had walked around Kress to reach the Tulia highway, trying to avoid anyone who might ask where I was going with the trumpet. Fortunately, the person who picked me up was a stranger, so initial apprehensions about being discovered before getting started turned out to be groundless. He dropped me off in downtown Tulia at the courthouse square at about dusk.

Tulia is mentioned here for a couple of reasons. For one thing, the humidity had turned to a wet, foreboding drizzle, foreboding because of previous "adventures" that had turned sour as a result of weather. Also, because I was alone in the rain, at night on a nearly deserted highway, and no choice but to keep on walking.

Once before, in nearly identical conditions, I had walked all the way from Lubbock to Littlefield. Another time it was from Ceta Canyon to Kress. Recalling those times, I again was as nervous as a hen at a coyote convention.

On the other hand, there was a world's championship heavyweight boxing match being broadcast that evening. I don't recall whether it was Dempsey or Tunney, or one of the matches between the two, but as I walked westward toward the Clovis highway I heard the announcer's every call through the open windows of houses. It was such an exciting fight I hardly noticed how wet I was getting.

I got lucky and two or three rides plus considerable walking put me into Clovis around midnight, which was pretty good for night-time hitch-hiking, but not so good otherwise, because now it was really raining and the town of Clovis was shut down for the night. It seemed a mile or more of slopping through mud, water and darkness out to where the highway began, only to find the highway itself wet, muddy and dark. Realization began to set in.

#

EPISODE FOUR

My luck was runnin' kind of muddy
and I was as unhappy
as a woodpecker in a petrified forest.

A Dark and Stormy Night

Before we begin the next episode, I must admit to you the feeling of some regret for ever starting this story. I worried that some of you would find the conditions described here most difficult to believe, or that your aging writer was ever that young, that poor and that foolish. But beyond that, how would our in-laws, friends, nieces, nephews, cousins and family members feel about these revelations now? Would we be banished from decent society?

I expressed those concerns to my wife, Wilsie, seeking her counsel before writing this episode. She merely smiled and came back in a few minutes with the following quote and said, "Go for it"!

"He that hath no
Fools, knaves or
Beggars in his
Family was begot
By a flash of
Lightning."
(anon.)

It surely looked like I was in for it again. Why do I keep getting into these situations, I asked myself. It's raining, I'm alone late at night on a deserted highway, wet, tired, hungry, no place to sit down, much less to lie down and rest, with the only option to keep on walking.

Even if a car did come by I could hardly be seen and who would stop for a wet, muddy stranger carrying a trumpet case anyway? They'd have to be crazy, too.

To put things in perspective, you need to visualize what rural highways in Texas and New Mexico were like in the early 30s. The meaning at that time was a road with bar ditches on either side and dirt from the ditches mounded up between and rolled flat to provide a "way" several inches higher than surrounding terrain; i.e., a "high way."

Through larger cities the surfaces were paved with brick, concrete or tarmac; in rural areas it was either left plain dirt, or a layer of caliche or clay was rolled on, acting as sort of a seal to protect the road bed when it rained.

(Editor's note: Caliche is a crust of calcium carbonate that forms on the stony soil of arid regions.)

These "high ways" went through buffalo wallows, lake beds and sometimes creeks, of course becoming submerged at times. Traffic was two-way, except for many bridges which were still only wide enough for one vehicle.

There were no traffic lanes, vehicles kicked up a lot of dust when it was dry, sank to their axles in mud with moderate rains, or skittered like pebbles on ice when on caliche or clay. And there was always the chance the road would drop under water in low areas.

Rather dejected and uncomfortable, and with deepening suspicions about my sanity for continuing to get into such predicaments, I kept on mucking along. I was as uncomfortable as a horse-thief at a hangin' bee.

Later, a dim light appeared, ahead and to the left. Coming closer I made out the word "Closed," and could see a few other lights, becoming drop lights over parking areas, and shadowy buildings. It was a motel! I just knew better than trying to wake the manager and strike a deal over 200 pennies for a room. He'd have called the cops. Besides, that was my whole stake and this was only the first night out. Those pennies had to last a long time.

Surveying the situation, it appeared that only a few units were occupied. Would the others be unlocked? Choosing the one farthest from the office I tried the door. Sure enough, it was not locked!

Pushing it open, I found a couple of matches in my pocket still dry enough to strike and took a quick look around. There was a bedstead and mattress, a dresser with mirror and a functional bathroom, but no pillows, sheets, covers, or towels.

Sometime later the rain stopped, and with dawn's early light I was up and out of there before anyone started stirring around. Getting back out on the highway I was rested, if only a couple of hours. I was as dry as a mud hen on a tin roof, clean as the heart of a preacher's wife, and feeling as optimistic as a gambler holding four aces and a wild card.

Providence had touched me.

#

EPISODE FIVE

I was as welcome
as lookin' at a pat straight flush.

Friends Found

It was only a few minutes before I was picked up. The fellow who gave me a ride lived in Fort Sumner, was a friend of Richard Herring's, and knew the grocery store where Richard worked. When we stopped at the store, Richard was in his white apron, sweeping the wooden front porch. After heartily greeting my new friend, Richard's attention shifted to me.

First his eyes lighted up, then a big smile of recognition as we clasped hands and were slapping each other's backs, then his jaw dropped and he looked worried. Later, he said it had dawned on him that maybe I'd want to stay with him and he had only a single room.

Richard said he knew both Roy and Crutch, that they shopped at his store. Roy's ranch was closer, only 33 miles southwest of Fort Sumner and both usually came into town about once a week.

But he also remembered that one of Roy's neighbors was in town that day and would stop back at the store later that afternoon to pick up an order. He was sure I could ride out to Roy's place with him.

In the meantime, Richard said he had some time coming that he'd like to take off and show me around Fort Sumner while we waited. But first, we went inside and he introduced me to his boss.

Then he went behind the counter and took out a large round of yellow cheese, cut off two generous slices and put them on paper plates, grabbed a few handfuls of crackers out of the cracker barrel, put a board across the top of the barrel and pulled up some chairs.

He told me to get some Cokes out of the cooler and we sat down to eat. I had the feeling he was used to young Texas teenagers showing up hungry. With that kind of meal there's a certain etiquette to be observed. One takes out his pocket knife, carefully wiping the blade on his pants leg, and uses that utensil for cutting and transporting cheese morsels to the mouth.

This is as good a spot as any to tell you something about Fort Sumner that most modern-day westerners probably don't know. Back in 1863 the famous scout, Kit Carson, was put in charge of an expedition to bring the Navajo Indians "under control."

The Navajos, along with the Apaches, were the most feared raiders and slavers of the region, preying on Spanish ranchers and the peaceful Hopi and Zuni tribes.

Carson systematically destroyed the great buffalo herds and other wild game, thus forcing the starving Navajos into submission. He took thousands of prisoners, transferring them to Fort Sumner, which is in eastern New Mexico. A so-called "peace treaty" was signed in 1868, returning the Navajos to their former lands in western New Mexico and Arizona. But, unfortunately, that didn't happen until after more than 1,000 Indians had died in captivity.

Fort Sumner remained an interesting town, and Richard was justly proud to show off the points of interest. For one thing, the legends of Billy the Kid and Sheriff Pat Garrett were still fresh in old-timer's minds and, for another, they had a spankin' new bridge across the Pecos River.

It was a beautiful thin structure of steel, gleaming in the sunlight, and Richard drove across it several times so we could admire it properly.

I've heard that legends keep on growing with time, and maybe that accounts for the number of houses, shacks, rooming houses, saloons and other buildings where Billy or the good sheriff, or both, allegedly fought, slept, ate, killed a man, partied, were holed up in, or whatever. Richard knew them all. Even the house where one of Billy's girl friends once lived was famous.

Outside of town a little way is a small, typical country cemetery where Billy is buried. Richard drove us there where we visited and paid our respects. Isn't it strange how we tend to honor the memories of infamous western outlaws as though they were heroes?

Billy the Kid's real name was NOT William H. Bonney ,as y'all have been misled to believe. It was claimed he killed 21 men by the time he was 21 years old, yet found friendly faces throughout middle New Mexico.

He had learned Spanish as a teen, and the Spanish-speaking of that state still talk about their affection for their "hero," Billy the Kid. People would hide him, give him money, help him escape and lie about his whereabouts.

Sheriff Pat Garrett, on the other hand, had it up-hill all the way. He was on Billy's trail for several years before finally catching him and shooting him dead.

The locals all seem to recollect that Garrett himself was killed not too long afterward in another shoot-out. T'warn't so!

More about that in a Texas minute.

#

EPISODE SIX

The undertaker was ridin' the
Devil's stallion to prosperity

Alias Billy the Kid

Let's turn this nag around for a spell, hole up in a friendly canyon and chaw a bit on Billy and Pat. Billy was not a westerner by birth. He was born in 1859 in a place that in recent years has become a dang sight more dangerous place than any shriveled spot under the western sun—New York City.

Until he was in his teens he was known as Henry McCarty. That sorta makes sense, I reckon, since his widowed mother's married name was McCarty.

His mother musta gotten the western wanderlust 'cause she took Henry and his brother and lit out fer the wide open spaces. That had to be sometime before he was 14 , 'cause that's how old Billy...er, ah...Henry...was when he signed as a witness—under his real name—to his mom's second marriage, in Santa Fe, N.M.

His stepfather was William Antrim. Later in Silver City, N.M., probably by more than coincidence, the famous outlaw-to-be sometimes called himself by the moniker of Billy, or Kid Antrim.

He was 15 when his mother died and he began living in bars and back alleys. He was in a bar on the outskirts of Fort Grant, N.M., when a brawlin', boozin' blacksmith decked him.

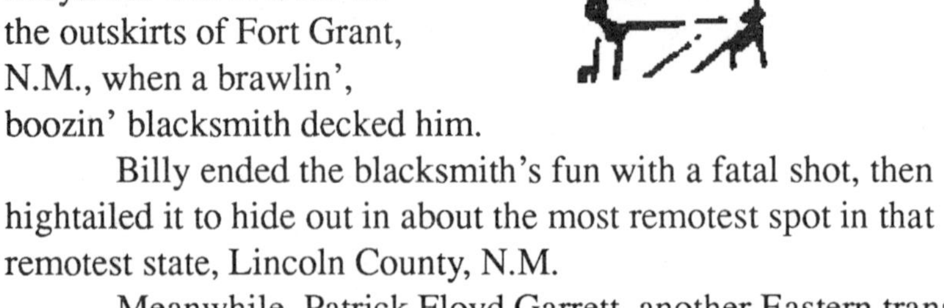

Billy ended the blacksmith's fun with a fatal shot, then hightailed it to hide out in about the most remotest spot in that remotest state, Lincoln County, N.M.

Meanwhile, Patrick Floyd Garrett, another Eastern transplant, had been born in Chambers County, Alabama, nine years before Billy was hatched. After heading fer the wide open spaces, among other work he did to keep the wolf from the door was to be

a buffalo hunter in Texas.

Somewhere along the trail, Pat and Billy became friends. But like a chaw o' tobacco, it didn't last long.

Pat was 30 when he "done got hisself elected," and pinned on the Lincoln County sheriff's badge. The next January (1881) he captured the Kid, who was tried and convicted at Mesilla. But the Kid snuffed out two guards and escaped from the county hoosegow.

That was on April 29, 1881. His life ended 76 days later, at the age of 22, in an ambush shortly after midnight on July 13, in a darkened bedroom of a military home in Fort Sumner. Pat Garrett had caught up with Billy, and thus both got caught up in the stuff of legends.

Garrett didn't die soon afterward, as is believed by some around these here parts. He became a tax collector and later a horse and cattle rancher.

But then he got into a dispute over some land ownership with Wayne Brazel, a New

Mexican rancher, and was fatally shot. That wasn't until 1908, 27 years after Billy had bit the dust. And only eight years before I was born.

Oh yeah, and Billy didn't kill 21 men as the lore goes. Records can be found to substantiate no more, possibly less, than eight gun-battle losers. But what the heck, that's still eight more losers than I'd want to be.

#

EPISODE SEVEN

When he got through breakin' those horses
they were as gentle as a frozen bull snake

Stark Naked

Leaving Fort Sumner for Roy's ranch, the terrain seemed a little rough and a whole lot up and down rocky hills, and we were traveling much, much faster than I thought reasonable or prudent. There may or may not have been an actual road under our wheels.

I never knew for sure, but I did feel the hand of providence keeping that vehicle upright and guiding it around obstacles in our path that could have meant certain death if we'd collided.

This was my first lesson about ranch life in New Mexico. Those crazy cowboys weren't afraid of anything. I mean not man, nor beast, nor machine, nor nature.

It seemed they enjoyed putting themselves in danger, perhaps seeing it as a challenge. I learned that lesson well; especially that they enjoy seeing others caught in dangerous situations, too, to my subsequent regret.

As we careened toward Roy's ranch it helped to get my mind off what looked like impending disaster and thinking about how Roy and his family might feel about my showing up unannounced.

I wished I'd let him know I was coming and asked his permission. It was doubtful they'd know me, as I'd grown nearly a foot taller. What would I say when they answered the door?

At dusk, my ride let me off at the gate, which led down a lane about a half-mile to their house. It was in a small valley and wasn't really visible from the road, just the windmill and some outbuildings. I kept regretting the imposition and embarrassment I was about to cause, and wishing I'd written or somehow let them know.

Around a bend in the lane appeared the rest of the windmill and outbuildings, including barns, tack room, privy, an earthen pond next to the windmill and a large, circular, stake corral containing 30 or 40 horses. The corral was like the Indians used to build, eight-foot-long saplings standing on end with the tops sharpened, and somehow lashed together to form a very sturdy enclosure that was as tight as a wood tick on a dog's tail.

Farther down around the bend I saw the house, almost hidden by a hill and just to my right. It was almost hidden because only the front of the house jutted out from the hill. The rest of the house was back into the hillside.

You could walk right up the hill and step off onto the roof. It was built of flat rock that was in sheets similar to flag stone. I'd seen a lot of it along creek beds and draws, and chinked with concrete.

I found out the walls were four feet thick. Lights were on inside and I knocked on the door.

Roy opened the door and greeted me as any hospitable New Mexican would a stranger on the doorstep, and peered at me for a bit before his eyes finally lighted up and he smiled, "Aren't you Aunt Lucy's boy? Come on in, boy, we're just sitting down to supper."

Roy was probably about 35 years old and his wife, Ora Lee, maybe about 30, although she looked no older than 16. They had two sons about 4 and 11. There was something very unusual about the younger one.

He was stark naked and brown as an Indian. I found that very curious.

They were asking me about family and friends in Kress and making idle chatter without pointedly asking the circumstances of my being there, which was appreciated. Finally, when I pushed my plate away and leaned back Roy asked if I was looking for a job. I told him I was, and he said that's fine, that he needed an extra hand for awhile.

To start, he had a guy hauling hay who needed some help and to be ready by 5 a.m. Fortune was smiling on me.

The bad news was that the hay to be hauled was away back up the other side of Fort Sumner. It was to be picked up in the field and hauled and stacked at a storage site in a small town there, not at Roy's place as I'd assumed.

Nobody had thought to tell me where we were going, or that we'd be gone a week or so, until I finally asked Tom, the driver, what was happening.

It was a job he and Roy had hired out to do. Did you ever handle hay bales? It's not for the tender-handed or the weak-of-back, I can assure you.

Riding toward the job site, Tom seemed in a talkative mood, and I was still curious about why that kid wasn't wearing any clothes. Tom told me that it was doctor's orders. One day about a year ago they realized they hadn't seen the youngster in a couple of hours and started searching, frantically.

Finally they found him floating face-down in the pond. They thought he was dead. He looked dead. They saw no indication of life, whatever.

But Roy kept working with him as his wife drove to the nearest doctor, which was probably in Fort Sumner. Somehow he started breathing again and they were able to save him.

After a long recovery they were allowed to bring him home, but the doctor told them the boy's lungs were severely damaged, that he'd be subject to respiratory disease until some healing and immunity was built up.

Lots of sunshine and fresh air was the prescription. Take him back to the ranch, strip all his clothes off and put him outside as much as possible so every square inch could absorb the sun's rays.

I asked Tom where we'd be staying when we got to the hay place. He grinned and said he'd thrown an extra sleeping bag in the truck, not to worry. There was a small general store there where we could eat, and if it rained or hailed we could get inside the truck. We'd make a light breakfast where we slept.

It's not much fun being caught on the blister end of a pitchfork, but hauling hay was pretty routine. That is, it doesn't require a master's degree in business administration or any great concentration, so there was lots of time for conversation, and Tom liked to talk.

I liked to listen, and I had questions, especially about Roy, his family, the ranch and ranching in general. What Tom told me is helpful in setting the stage for this story.

According to Tom, the corral full of horses back at the ranch was an important second revenue source for Roy. Those were wild horses, wilder'n a turpentined cat when he got 'em. They had been captured by different ranchers and turned over to Roy for breaking and training.

It's a lot easier to catch 'em than to break 'em, and Roy was known for his special talent. The horses he turned out were in demand. I later watched him working horses and he really was good, very good. He kept them and worked with them for six weeks or longer before they "graduated."

#

EPISODE EIGHT

A snake-bit man
is afraid of a rope

Dirty, Smelly and Dangerous

Roy was runnin' cattle on about 30 sections of land. About half was his and the other half leased from the government. It was not a large ranch for that area because it took about 10 acres per head for adequate grazing.

I've been trying to remember Roy's brand. I thought it was Bar S. Doing a little backup research for this book, I contacted a fellow I know at the research desk at Amarillo Central Library.

Well, there was no record of a Bar S or S Bar ranch, anywhere. He did find Bar S Bar ranch in Texas with three addresses, and Bar S business names in Texas and three other states.

I guess we can only conclude that Roy's brand was never officially registered. There were so many small ranches, probably only the biggest and most famous even bothered to register brands, because the primary purpose was to sort out your cattle from your neighbors' stock. And to tell you the truth, I never heard any stories about disputes arising over unregistered brands while I was cowboying with Roy.

The ground on Roy's ranch was rocky, and grass grew in sparse clumps, with much more ground showing than grass. And finally, well water throughout that part of the state was so "gyppy" it was unfit for human consumption. It was so mean-tastin' it ran uphill and wanted to stay in the jug.

Drinking it resulted in dire consequences, but it didn't bother livestock at all. Ranchers without access to fresh-water streams caught their drinking and cooking water in cisterns. More about that later.

Ultimately, you may get accustomed to blistered, bleeding hands and an aching back from loading and unloading hay bales all day, and even going to the little store and eating cheese and crackers twice a day, every day. But there's one thing that really bothered me.

It makes me nervous just to tell about it. That was sleeping on the ground in rattlesnake country. Skunks are bad enough, but they aren't necessarily fatal. Rattlesnakes are.

Those creepy, cold-blooded boogers just love to crawl into your sleeping bag on a chilly night and cuddle up against you to keep warm. So, sleeping was a challenge. You're watching the ground around you in the moonlight, and shadows start movin'.

You doze off only to awaken in a panic because of a big wrinkle, you are afraid to move or turn over, and when you awaken in the morning you do so very quietly, gently and carefully so as not to disturb a potential bedmate. Gives ya a funny feelin' running up your spine, like bristles on a wild boar. That feelin' is enough to make even the hair of a buffalo robe stand up and take notice.

It does not help that your hay buddy regales you with a lifetime of stories about horrors suffered by friends and late friends at the hands (?) of rattlesnakes in their bedrolls, or of failed attempts to keep them out, such as lariats or rocks circled around the bed.

Needless to say, after seein' and killin' plenty of rattlers in the fields during our hay mission, this Texas tenderfoot slept very little and very lightly the entire time. I escaped having any bedroll encounters at that time. There was one at another time and location, but I'll tell you about it later.

Out in the hayfield was a different situation—not recommended for the fainthearted. The hay had been lying there quite awhile and every bale you picked up had small animals or something crawly under it, hanging on to the bottom, or inside. And some of the bales were pretty smelly, too, and even slimy with mildew and mold. By the time we finished, both Tom and I had gotten about as dirty and smelly as the hay. How long can you go without a bath, anyway?

We were kind of keeping our distance from each other, you can be sure. Both my pairs of pants were out at the knees and threadbare from there up, my shirt was in tatters, and my feet smelled to high heaven. You can't imagine two more miserable-looking, filthy, unkempt excuses for humanity than Tom and me when we were finally through with that job and had crawled into the truck and pointed it back toward the ranch.

But I was satisfied, maybe a bit smug. I had survived what must have been the ultimate test with flying colors. Boy, did that assumption ever turn out to be wrong! Tom was either as anxious to get back as I was or couldn't stand the way I smelled much longer because instead of following the road around the ranch he opened a gate in the fence and went barreling down the hillside to the house.

We never knew whether the cows smelled hay residue in the truck, or thought it was their mother, but here they came. They followed us all the way back. Tom dropped me and went off somewhere, and the first thing I wanted was a bath. It was imperative! Roy had a bathroom, which he'd added to the front, and it had a big old porcelain bathtub, but that was the only fixture, and it wasn't plumbed.

Like most ranches, there was hot and cold water. That is, hot in the summer and cold in the winter. No water in and no water out. You had to fill the tub with pails of water from the pond and drain it by bailing the water out.

By this time, my trousers were shot. When I got through, Roy's wife had laid out fresh pants for me. Her pants! A little full, but they worked. I wore her pants from then on.

In fact, I wore them until I got back to Kress. Can you imagine? It was either that or my underwear, but by then my shorts were so beat they wouldn't stay up without the pants, anyway.

#

EPISODE NINE

There ain't a hoss can't be rode.
There ain't a man can't be throwed.

From Bareback to Saddle

At supper, Roy asked if I could ride a horse. I assured him I was practically born on a horse, but bareback, since we didn't have a saddle. He smiled, weakly, and said he'd fix me a saddle. Tomorrow he wanted me to help him break some of those horses.

Again my sleep was troubled. I wished they'd stop telling me at supper what was in store the next day. I tended to worry. Would I ride the orneriest horse out there to a standoff? Or would I be thrown to the top of that fence and just hang head-down across it while everyone rolled on the ground with laughter?

Well, that's not the way it went. I told you Roy had a special technique that was greatly admired. He had four or five regular, trained cow-horses in the corral with the wild ones who sort of looked up to them as resident group leaders. The monkey-see, monkey-do type of thing, hopefully. It works, up to a point.

I roped, bridled and saddled a tame horse, and the wild ones watched. I got in the saddle and was promptly thrown.

They watched that, too. Roy roped, bridled and saddled a wild one, who fought at every step.

Roy finally got on board and lasted about four jumps before he was thrown. They also watched that. So far, the students were running the classroom.

We eventually got Roy back in the saddle by tying up one of his horse's hind legs. When we cut it loose the horse tried everything in the book to unseat Roy, including trying to rub him off on the corral fence, but Roy stuck with him.

Finally, the horse simmered down to a trot and was responding to the reins. In the meantime, I had managed to get back on my horse.

"Come on, Kid," Roy yelled, "let us through the gate. Let's go out and ride the range awhile."

Despite what you may have been led to believe to the contrary, I did get the gate open, get Roy and me and our mounts through it, and get it closed again without letting any of the other horses out. Honest!

I was in Roy's wife's saddle. Roy had lengthened the stirrups to fit my long legs, and it felt quite comfortable... for awhile.

Saddles were made for work; a coiled rope from the saddle horn, which you used often, pouches for tools used in simple fence and windmill repairs or to help cows having birthing problems, medicines for sick animals and maybe a sandwich for lunch. Tied in a roll on the back of the saddle—if you're smart like a bunkhouse rat—is foul weather gear and a sleeping bag. Saddles then were as essential as pickups now.

My horse knew far more about handling stock than I did and he was making me look pretty good, but I couldn't throw a rope for anything. I definitely needed to develop some skills in that area, 'cause skill throws more weight than strength.

I was thoroughly enjoying riding and talking with Roy while enjoying scenery and doing routine cowboy stuff. He told me about ranch life.

"It's hard, very hard, especially on women"—and then he casually asked whether I'd told my Mom and Bobbie Lee where I was going when I left home.

I had to tell him no. I was feeling badly about that. He said, "Well, I mailed them a letter last night."

#

EPISODE TEN

Ya can't drive a range-raised horse
over a rattlesnake.

Fatal Fangs

Suddenly, both horses shied and snorted.

"Rattlesnake!" Roy yelled. "Kill him, Kid, before he gets away."

"How?" I yelled back.

"Jump off your horse on to his head," he screamed. " I can't, I'd have to tie up my horse again."

"Hell, I can't, either," I shot back. "I'm not wearin' boots, I'm wearin' Oxfords."

Roy was getting steamed.

"Hurry! Get down and kill him. Hit him with a rock, a mesquite grub, anything. He's getting away and he'll kill a cow or something!"

I jumped down and kept one eye on the snake as it slithered between clumps of grass on sunbaked and rockless clay, while I searched for a grub with the other. I found one, about 14 inches long.

I considered: What were the chances of killing a five-foot-long rattler with only a 14-inch-long mesquite grub? And not get bitten myself? I threw the grub and missed as the snake went down a hole.

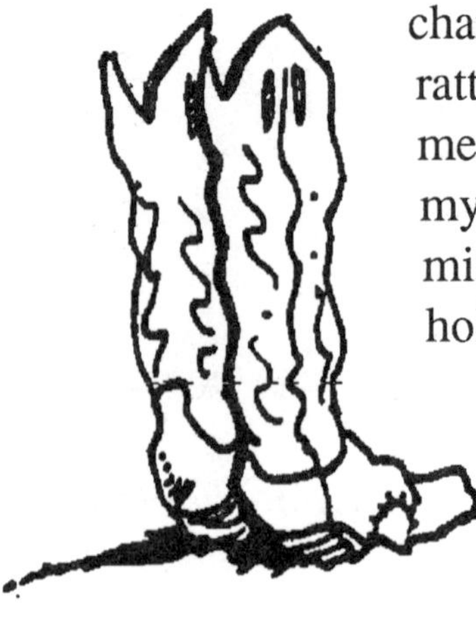

The rest of the day Roy was pretty angry. He was in a sod-pawin', horn-tossin' mood, and kept wondering out loud why I couldn't have somehow killed that snake.

Sometimes I'd see him looking at me and shaking his head. I wished I had tried to jump on the snake.

I thought I'd rather have been lying on the prairie racked with pain and dying from snake venom than to be facing Roy's disapproval. I was not very proud of myself, either.

It was a long day. When we finally got back and went in for supper Roy's wife had bad news. One of Roy's close friends had died that day from rattlesnake bite.

(I'm not making it up, this actually did happen as I'm telling it.)

A couple days before, the friend had jumped off his horse onto a rattlesnake's head. He killed the snake, but its fangs punctured through the snake's head, broke off and embedded in the fellow's boot heel.

When he took the boots off that night the broken fangs scratched his hand. He didn't realize what had happened until he was deathly ill and it was already too late for a doctor.

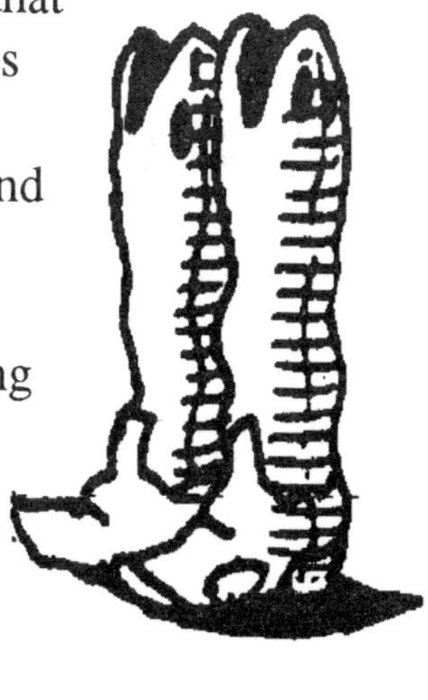

As the story unfolded, I couldn't help noticing Roy watching my face and his own expression changing. That wasn't the first incident of someone dying from fangs stuck in a boot heel, or for that matter, from someone jumping and missing a snake's head. Tom had told me up in the hay country how cowboys liked to kill snakes that way, and what can happen sometimes.

Then Roy told about our snake episode that day and how he got excited and tried to put my life on the line. He said I showed a lot better judgment than he did, and how glad he was that I had ignored his orders.

At bedtime that night, Roy shook my hand, real hard and looked me in the eyes. He didn't say anything.

He didn't need to.

#

EPISODE ELEVEN

In cow country, every prairie dog hole
kin swaller hooves n' money,
every creek is a river,
every loudmouth in a bar is a liar, and
every moonshiner is your neighbor.

Killin' the Town

Roy and his family sort of accepted me as a member after that, which made me feel really good. Days were spent as before, with Roy riding a fresh bronco every day as part of their training, and usually one or both of us would get thrown. That part was getting to be almost routine.

I guess it just proves that a bronc rider should be light in the head and heavy in the saddle.

We were fixing fences and other stuff and becoming quite close. Then, one evening when we got home his wife had killed a big rattler on their front porch...shot his head off with Roy's .45 Long Colt.

Wow! I was impressed. But, we figured the mate was still around, and you can't have a couple of small boys, one of them naked, playing around in a yard full of rattlesnakes.

So, we spent the next day policing the whole yard area, removing brush, weeds, trash, debris, anything that could hide a snake. We looked for snakes and even holes that might contain snakes. We also thoroughly inspected and cleaned the earthen cellar. Roy pointed with pride to several shelves holding many bottles of homemade brew.

Remember, this was about 1930. Prohibition hadn't been repealed yet and what he was showing me down there was very illegal.

I stepped out of the cellar for something and saw the county sheriff's vehicle coming down the lane.

"Quick, Roy, get out of the cellar and close the door", I shouted. "The sheriff's coming."

"It's OK", Roy yelled back.

The sheriff got out and nodded to me and went directly to the cellar and down the steps. They came up a minute later carrying three open long-necks and handed one to me.

Sitting in the shade, the sheriff said he had dropped by to tell us the county prairie dog abatement man was coming the next day to go over the ranch and could the Kid help him. The Kid could.

About dawn the next morning the prairie dog guy arrived and after coffee we set out on our mission. His vehicle was several years old, probably a forerunner to station wagons. It was based on a Ford or Chevy two-door sedan body, and where the back scat should have been it was converted to light cargo space, and where the rear window should have been was an access door. It was rigged for rough terrain, including six-ply tires and self-sealing tubes. Inside were his wide-mouthed metal containers of prairie dog poison. It was then that I connected the term "abatement" with "going over the ranch."

That bothered me. I told him to pull over, I didn't want to go out "abating" prairie dogs without good reason. So we got out and talked and he convincingly ticked off the reasons:

a) They spread and populate quickly, a prairie dog town

can cover 1 to 20 acres and unless stopped could cover the whole ranch,

b) If cows or horses step into the holes they usually break a leg and have to be destroyed, and

c) Many of the holes contain rattlesnakes. They like to nest down there and raise their young.

That last reason was the clincher. I said, "C'mon, let's go out and abate those rascals."

#

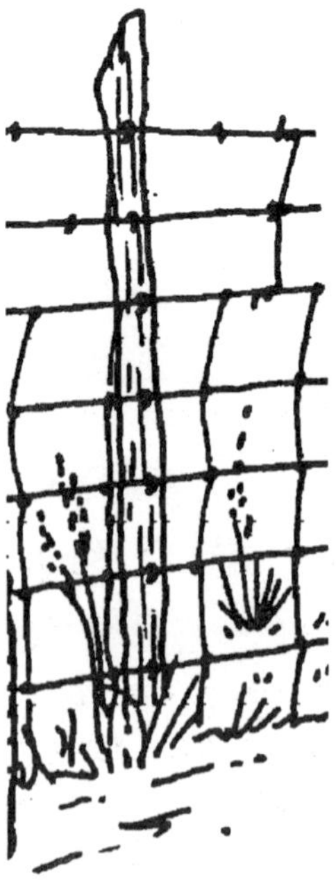

EPISODE TWELVE

Prairie dog towns
had more inhabitants
than cowboy towns

A Stinkin' Job

I want to interrupt this story for a related incident: As I was writing this, I heard on the news that movie actress Greer Garson had died, and as she played a role later in this story, it seems appropriate to go ahead and tell you now.

In the early 1950's, Vivian and I scheduled our vacations to include Santa Fe for the Fiesta. Six of our relatives were to join us a few days later. Prior to their arrival, we were having dinner one evening at La Fonda when Miss Garson and her party came in and sat near us. It was a jovial gathering, Fiesta Time, and pretty soon some of her people came over and introduced themselves.

They seemed surprised when they heard the name Skipworth and asked us to sit with them while waiting for our food. They wanted us to meet Miss Garson. She also showed surprise when introduced, as did the others. Well, Greer Garson and her husband owned a big ranch in New Mexico, which was news to me, and her foreman was none other than one of Roy Skipworth's two sons. (I don't know whether it was the naked one or the other one.)

Because Skipworth was a rare name, they guessed we must be related. They talked at length about the young man, as if they really liked him, and they had other news. Sadly, the older brother had been killed in World War ll.

Roy and his wife were in Fort Sumner by this time. He was the county sheriff. Sometime along in the early 1980's, I got further word that Roy's son had retired, and that Miss Garson had built him a nice retirement home with some acreage on one corner of her ranch.

The prairie dog guy (let's call him Pete) and I bounced along, crisscrossing the ranch many times, stopping at prairie dog towns and doing our thing. I hadn't dreamed there were so many. The ranch was riddled with them, some 10 acres or more in diameter. I was the shovel man.

Typically, Pete chose a "main" hole and I covered all the holes around it with dirt while he got one of those cans out of the car. When I was ready, he pulled a saturated cotton ball, about baseball

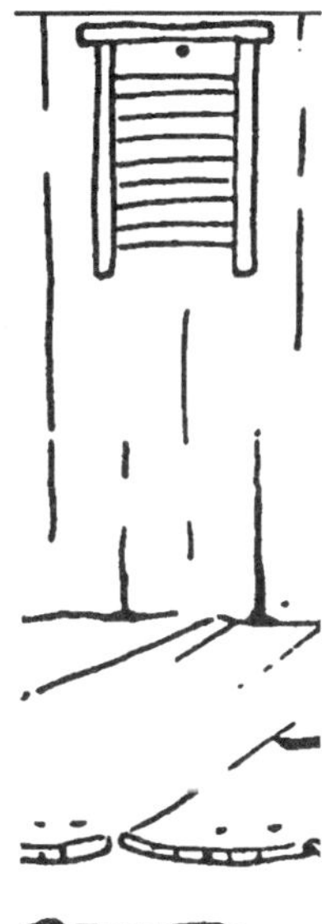

size, out of the can, tossed it into the "main" hole and dropped in a lighted match. When it went "Whoof" I covered that hole, too.

He was gassing them, humanely, and taking care of the rattlesnakes, too. I could go for that! Yes, not all of the snakes were in the holes where they belonged.

We moved from "main" hole to "main" hole throughout each town and from town to town, but frequently after we got back in his car I could smell the most awful odor. I kept looking sideways at Pete, wondering if he was ill, or had a major digestive problem, or if it was something he'd eaten, although we'd had the same thing which was very little. Then, I thought maybe he'd had a slight "accident," but he seemed unaware that anything was wrong, while I was starting to get sick.

When we stopped I kept sniffing around the truck and finally found the source. It was coming from those cans. When we returned to the car each time, his gloves were still wet and smelly from the poison! I never told him about my suspicions.

We finished about dusk and returned to the house, and Pete told Roy that the Kid was a real good worker. Roy liked that, and put his hand on my shoulder as we told Pete goodbye.

At supper that night Roy thanked me for helping Pete and told me that I'd be riding alone the next day. He was getting behind with the broncos, and he'd tell me in the morning about some things he wanted me to check on and to do out there.

I was going to solo!

#

EPISODE THIRTEEN

On the range, saddles are pillows
for either end.

Findin' Nesters

We found a shocking sight at the corral the next morning. One of the wild horses, a beautiful stallion that had been delivered only a day or so before, was dead.

He had apparently been spooked by something during the night and had tried to jump over that eight-foot-high fence. He had impaled himself on those pointed stakes.

He was just hanging there. It made us sick. Roy said nothing like that had ever happened before.

Now the rest of the horses were scared and nervous and we were afraid they'd try to jump the fence, too.

We finally got them calmed down by walking among them and talking to them, rubbing or patting the ones that would let us, and putting out some more feed.

But getting that dead horse down off the fence and disposing of his body was quite a task. It was near mid-day when Roy got to his bronc busting and I got out on the range.

It was nice riding alone. It was like getting your training wheels removed and being accepted as a cowboy and a man. I was even feeling at home in the saddle after having been strictly a bareback rider before. You could rope and work from a saddle; you couldn't do that bareback.

For me, it was still easier to ride bareback and was easier to mount and dismount. All you did was throw a leg over the horse's shoulder and slide off. But the downside was when you and your horse both start sweating and your seat and legs get soaked and you start breaking out with prickly heat in the affected areas. That's bad.

Now I was feeling as happy and comfortable in the saddle as a puppy with two tails. There's one big disadvantage to saddles I should mention. To dismount when using a saddle, the safest way is to remove both feet from the stirrups, place both hands on the pommel, and slide to the ground, the reins being retained in the left hand. This eliminates the danger of being dragged should the horse start while the rider still had his left foot in the stirrup using the normal way of dismounting.

Well, that may be appropriate for rodeo or bronc riders, but it's totally inappropriate for range hands. A poor old, dog-tired, stove-up cowboy is going to get down one leg at a time. He'll still be holding the reins in one hand. Besides, it'd scare hell out of his horse if he vaulted from the saddle.

Among the things Roy wanted me to do were first to check

on some nesters he'd seen moving in on the leased land. Roy was concerned about their welfare, especially whether they had food and water, and he told me to tell them it was OK to slaughter a beef if they were hungry. This was totally foreign to anything I'd heard before about how ranchers treated nesters, but I was going to do it.

There was another thing he wanted done, too. He'd noticed a fence down and some of the neighbors' stock mixing in our herd.

I was to weed them out and drive them back across the fence and then fix the fence. That sounded simple enough, I thought, even for a born-again cowboy wearing a woman's pants and riding in a woman's saddle.

I found the nesters where Roy said they'd be, and they were rather nervous until I told them Roy sent me. They had heard that Roy was pretty nice. I found out later there were five or six nester families living on his ranch, and he was trying to help all of them as he could.

Roy was the kind of guy who spread happiness where he went, not when.

This was a family with several kids ranging from about two into the middle teens. They were all in tatters and looking hungry. I felt so sorry for them because they were good, honest people.

Remember, this was the Great Depression. People were destitute, banks failed, savings gone, factories closed, crops rotting in fields, mortgages foreclosed, the bleakest of all times.

Survival just until things maybe got better was life's foremost challenge.

This family was trying to fix things up and live on the site of a former nester. When I told them Roy said they could butcher a beef, they couldn't believe this punk kid. But I convinced them, and I never before saw such deep gratitude.

They were my new best friends. I guess it's true that a friend in need is a friend, indeed.

When I left to round up the neighbor's cows and fix the fences they made me promise to return soon and eat and visit with them. As I looked back before rounding a hill they were still waving.

#

EPISODE FOURTEEN

Whenever yer in doubt,
let yer horse do the thinkin'

Horse Sense

Riding along, looking for the fence break, I was feeling good about things. When you're a kid you notice adult attitudes, and you kind of know when you're being pushed forward into more responsibility and trust, and being treated more as an equal.

It had been awhile since they'd called me the Kid or the Tenderfoot, and I liked that, and liked what I was doing, more than anything I'd ever done. One of the things I enjoyed most was working with a well-trained cow horse, and mine was.

Somebody told me, "Remember, your horse has been a cowboy all his life." It's true. He knows more about handling cattle than his rider ever will.

When he senses what you want done he does it. All you do is sit on his back and smile and be ready to lean into turns and squeeze with your legs—when he breaks into a run or stops suddenly—to avoid falling off.

It's a real pleasure to team up with a good horse. I loved it. I found where the fence was down and, as Roy suspected, quite a few head, a hundred or more, were on our side and were scattered and mixed among our herd.

The older steers and cows were willing to be cut out and driven back. But the yearlings thought it was a big fun game, and a couple of old bulls tried to fight us. So, I did what any good cowboy with problems would do: I let the horse take charge.

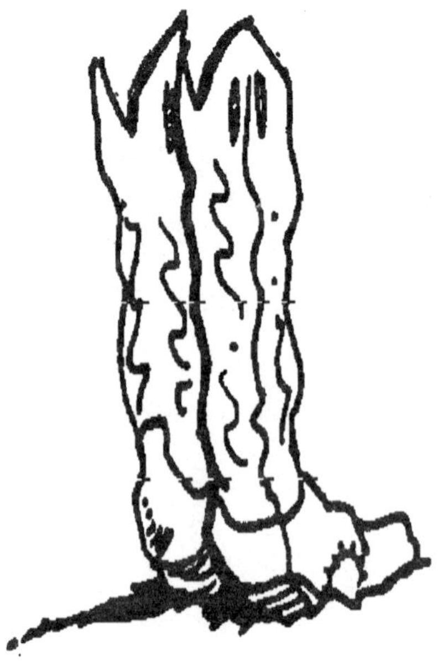

Suddenly, a yearling cut back like greased lightning and headed for the hills. My horse wheeled and was right after him at a full run. The next few seconds were an unbelievable eternity, but believe it!

Another quick turn and we were into one of those prairie dog towns where I'd covered some of the holes. The horse couldn't see the other holes. A front leg dropped into a hole.

We both went down, head first, my feet under his chest. I'd mentally written him off before we hit the ground.

My mind instantly raced ahead of what was actually occurring. I thought, "This wonderful horse with a broken leg, what will I do? Miles from any house, I can't shoot him and I can't leave him like this.")

After the initial impact, momentum threw me forward over his head about another 15 feet. I was laying there, partially dazed, and upset by the fate I thought I'd brought on my horse.

Previous feelings of warmth over acceptance as a real cowboy had evaporated. What I felt like now was a little boy, wanting to bury his face in the dirt and cry his heart out.

Then I felt nuzzling around my head and face. It was my horse, standing over me and trying to get me up. I couldn't believe it! That horse was concerned about me!

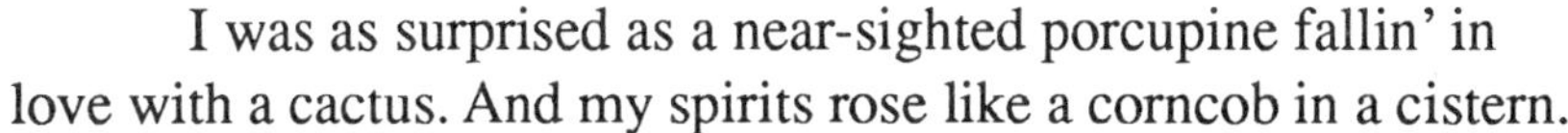

I was as surprised as a near-sighted porcupine fallin' in love with a cactus. And my spirits rose like a corncob in a cistern.

There he was, standing and nuzzling me, those big brown eyes so contrite and apologetic, like it was all his fault. Hey! He was STANDING! On all four feet!

His leg wasn't broken! I jumped up and hugged him and walked him about, watching, and he never limped or even flinched. Amazing!

It was only then that I noticed my shoes were missing. Remember the Oxfords? I found them where we hit the ground, one on either side, and something else that was equally unbelievable. At every eyelet on both shoes the laces had broken!

Twenty breaks in each shoelace.

Apparently, the sudden pressure on my feet between the ground and horse's chest had done it. Not a piece longer than two inches.

While knotting enough pieces together to hold my shoes on I did some thinking about the day's events. It started on such a sad note with the wild horse killing himself, then the euphoric feeling while riding the range alone and being sort of a hero to the nester family.

I learned about humility that day, and what had to be Divine Intervention. My horse could have suffered a broken neck or leg, and so could I, or at least a crushed foot or ankle. Neither of us was hurt, and my horse and I had become close buddies.

#

EPISODE FIFTEEN

If your horse knew
how puny you really are,
he'd stomp you to death
and head fer the hills.

Hidin' the Whiskey

That night Roy told me to pack a sleeping bag and whatever I needed to be gone a couple of weeks. Next morning we were to ride over to Don's ranch to meet Crutch and Jack Skipworth and some other neighbors to help Don with his annual roundup and branding.

Don and his wife were family friends and a neighboring rancher of Crutch and Roy. The ranch was the largest of five ranches being operated in New Mexico by Don's family. One leg of it lay between Roy and Crutch's ranches, and in total it was probably larger than both their ranches combined.

Don was a young man in his early twenties, and had been married less that a year. Typical of the times, when the family scion took a wife, the rich papa moved him and his new bride onto the flagship of all his properties, and into its spacious residence, which resembled a governor's mansion.

You'd think a happy-ever-after in princessdom would be assured, wouldn't you? But there were some really interesting pitfalls in the road. First, old Don grew up a cow-man and he was as common as dirt.

Second, his bride's family was Eastern Money and she was from a fancy finishing school. Her family was reputed to be wealthier than Don's. And finally, Don must have been falling-down drunk when he gave a solemn promise to his betrothed that

he would stop drinking. It appears that Don had bottle fever.

The amazing thing to all of us was how Don could remember, throughout that vast ranch, which fence posts had a bottle of rotgut at their base.

Hot whiskey on a hot day is only for the very desperate, I'd think, but then Don was desperate. He couldn't drink around that big fancy house or fine wife. Most of the time, she pretended he really had stopped drinking.

Synopsis: We had gone over to newly-married, trying-to-stop-drinking Don's big ranch to help him, along with other neighbors, do his annual roundup and branding. Ranching had been Don's life, but this was an entirely new experience. It was his ranch, his stock, he was boss, and he and his new wife were hosting. She had no experience at all. She was a city girl.

They had a few problems to work out. But typical of the Old West, friends and neighbors quickly gathered around to help and advise; wives counseling the bride on housebreaking the husband, bedroom etiquette including how to fake a headache,

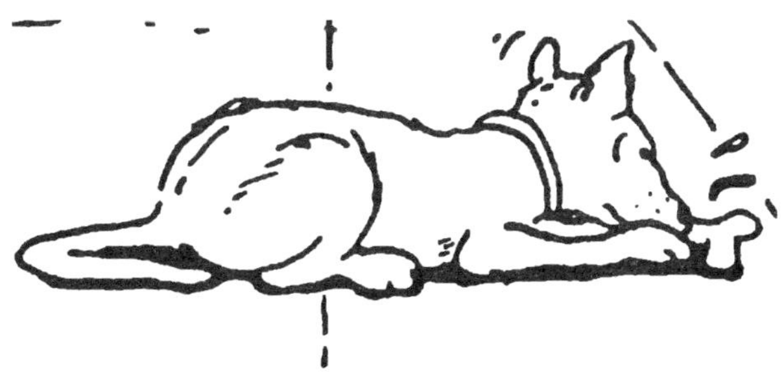

kitchen tips and how to become boss without his knowing it. You know! Girl talk!

The same with old Don; how to let your wife know who's boss, how to act in the bedroom, including what to do about her headache, going out with the boys, bringing the boys home, and how to continue hiding his drinking. Western folk loved practical jokes and a lot of the advice for both was designed to have dire consequences.

#

EPISODE SIXTEEN

He may not have been drownin' in drink
but he managed to keep well-irrigated.

Drunk in the Saddle

I hesitate to go further, because of the family nature of these true tales, but I'll mention just one example. Somebody advised old Don that it was OK to use Mentholatum if he couldn't find the Vaseline. I guess he did, because they were two angry people.

(What keeps making me think of frogs on a hot skillet?)

Of course, I didn't understand most of what they were talking about until I got older, and I've had lots of chuckles looking back. Don and his wife must have been as naive as they come.

Corrals near the house were always for horses. Unless as some ranchers did, you kept a couple of milk cows, too.

Corrals for handling cattle were always about as far away from the house as you could get them, for obvious reasons. Sometimes that would be 10 or 15 miles and as close as possible to transportation.

The object of the roundup is to scour the entire range, locate and cut out unbranded calves and yearlings, and drive them toward the corral. You drove the mothers, too, if they were still nursing. Oddly, I thought, some still nursed their yearlings until the next calf came.

Several cowboys are posted near the corral and they contain the affected cattle close by in a herd, where they can graze and have water while waiting. They hold the cattle there in an increasingly larger herd until all target cattle have been brought up and all hands ready. Then in small, manageable groups you drive them inside the corral—mothers too—for branding and other activities, none very pleasant for the recipient.

Today, this kind of work would give the term, "Labor Intensive," a bad name, but more about that later. Early the first day we all met at the corral, unloaded our sleeping bags and gear, laid plans and received assignments.

There were probably 25 or 30 of us, including Don's resident cowboys. The ranch was divided into quadrants and a team assigned to each, with three or four men remaining at the corral, including the cook. Each team would drive its unbranded cattle to the corral at night and turn them over to the herders. The wives would meet us out there with dinner from the ranch house and we'd all eat together, picnic style.

The cook had breakfast for us so early that we were already gone before daylight. If you wanted, you stuffed a couple of biscuits in your saddlebag for lunch. That's why cowboys—hired hands on horseback paid to out-think cows—are skinny as a desert grasshopper.

Crutch and Jack Skipworth, Roy, Don and I were on the same team. We had difficulty keeping Don away from fence posts where he had whiskey bottles hidden.

Did you ever try drinking bootleg whiskey that's almost at the boiling point? We did, several times that first day—just to be sociable of course—but Don got pretty tanked up.

He was so drunk that one of the funniest things I ever saw happened. Don and his horse took off on a wild gallop after a yearling, Don swinging his rope like crazy. He cast the loop and it was so big the yearling ran through it.

Don stepped off into thin air, the horse still at full gallop, and he hit the ground and tumbled end-over-end several times, then somersaulted at least another 15 times. We thought he must be hurt bad, but he got up and started running after his horse.

We caught it for him and got him back in the saddle. He just laughed and guessed he'd sort of lost track of what he was doing.

I was as happy as a flea in a doghouse to be on the same horse that had stepped in the prairie dog hole. He'd been "my" horse ever since and we had become real friends. I petted him a lot, and he whinnied at me and followed me around when we weren't working.

When we were working, he was careful with me, making sure I didn't fall off. It was a special bond. I guess we each felt guilty for letting the other fall.

I don't think there are any really easy jobs in a roundup, but you do get to work with some very interesting characters who don't mind letting you experience some of the more unrewarding pursuits. Since cattle have an obsession to stay in the herd, as you separate the unbranded and in most cases their moms, they keep trying to break away and rejoin the herd.

Somebody has to keep that from happening, which turned out to be Jack and me. The other men worked the main herd and brush, while trying to keep Don away from fence posts.

#

EPISODE SEVENTEEN

Sweat never drowned anyone,
but it sure is a waste o' booze.

Jack, the Roper

Jack was an excellent cowboy and had done well in local rodeos. His aim was the big time and he was always practicing, especially with his rope. It was constantly in his hand, much to my regret because he loved moving targets.

We'd take off at full run after a wayward calf and the next thing I'd know Jack's rope would have caught one of my horse's legs and Jack would be reeling with laughter. You and your horse were his hostage. Running, turning, stopping, you had to stay inside of his rope's length or be thrown. You were linked until he was ready to call it off. Then, pretty soon, always unexpectedly and at high speed, he'd do it again.

A lariat ranges from 33 to 37 feet long, according to personal choice, and one end stays firmly fixed to the saddle horn. There wasn't much margin for error on either end.

I was getting frustrated and as cross as a snapping turtle

before finally realizing that Jack was so highly skilled he wasn't really trying to dump me. He was just having fun. But my horse was having a blast. He thought it was a big game and he wasn't about to let me be taken down. He kept Jack busy trying to keep tension on the rope as we maneuvered about him and I'd swear he was laughing. But it was a very nervous game.

After a sandwich and rest break one day we started out again, Jack in front. I was not a good roper yet, but I took the rope down, shook out a loop and started gently swinging it as we closed in. My horse got so excited he could hardly stand it. We were about to be the ropers instead of the ropees and he was almost jumping for joy. Ever so silently we stole up behind Jack and I threw the loop.

It was a lucky throw and before Jack knew what was happening, the loop settled over his hat and shoulders. At about the same time my horse pulled back, pinning Jack's arms to his waist, and enough off balance that he had to grab the saddle horn with both hands to keep from being unseated.

My horse and I were having the time of our lives. We'd go left and right of Jack, ahead and behind, my horse keeping the rope tight enough to keep old Jack's arms pinned, off-balance and pulling leather. He was yelling and cussing up a storm.

You see, he knew I wasn't that good, and could easily have accidentally hurt him. I guess if he had known it was my horse doing the driving and pestering he'd have been less uneasy. We kept it going until my horse seemed to have gotten his rightful revenge, Jack cussing and hollering all the way, before letting the rope go slack.

If Jack had done all the things to me he said he was going to, somebody else would have had to write this story. But, I'll tell you this, Jack was the greatest at roping one foot of a speeding animal that I've heard of. Maybe in the whole world. Interestingly, however, for some reason he never threw a rope at one of my horse's feet again.

#

EPISODE EIGHTEEN

So, what is bigger'n Dallas?

Gettin' Spruced Up

We always looked forward to the women showing up at the corral in the evening about the time we drove our calves in for the night. They would have gathered earlier at Don's house and put finishing touches on what they had brought, made a basket of fresh biscuits and sometimes even frozen some ice cream.

I had mentioned it was like a picnic, but it was really more like a social. Everything was piping hot that was supposed to be and the cold stuff was cold. There would be platters of fried chicken, steak and okra, bowls of gravy, mashed potatoes, black-eyed peas and pinto beans.

Maybe someone had also made cornbread and there were relishes, pies and cakes. If they had been to town and gotten ice to make ice cream, we also had iced tea and an option of that round-up coffee...I'll tell you about that coffee, later.

* * *

I just remembered a self-explanatory expression that's common around this part of the country:

"Don't ever ask a buxom lady what's bigger than Dallas."

Okay, enough said on that subject!

* * *

One evening, someone mentioned they hadn't been to town on a Saturday night in a long time and most everybody said, "Hey, we haven't, either." They all thought everybody going to town together was a grand idea.

The roundup would be finished by then, they wanted a break before starting the really hard work of branding and besides, Don's ranch hands could look after the stock at the corral while we were gone.

"What'll we do with the kids," some of them wondered, and they got that settled. Everything was decided and the planning began for Saturday night in town. I was happy about it, too.

By now I really needed shoe strings, as I only had enough

knotted string left from that fall to go through two eyelets on each shoe, and I'd been out of smoking tobacco and cigarette papers for weeks. Besides, I'd been leading a rigorous life and felt I deserved a night on the town.

By now, most of the calves and yearlings had been rounded up and were being held outside the corral by Don's riders. The rest of us were riding far and wide, combing the whole ranch again for any stragglers. Our team was pretty much riding together, leisurely, and making occasional stops at Don's special fence posts, and having a pretty good time.

Tomorrow night was the night, the BIG SATURDAY NIGHT. I guess we were really getting primed for it, doing a lot of talking and joking and kidding around.

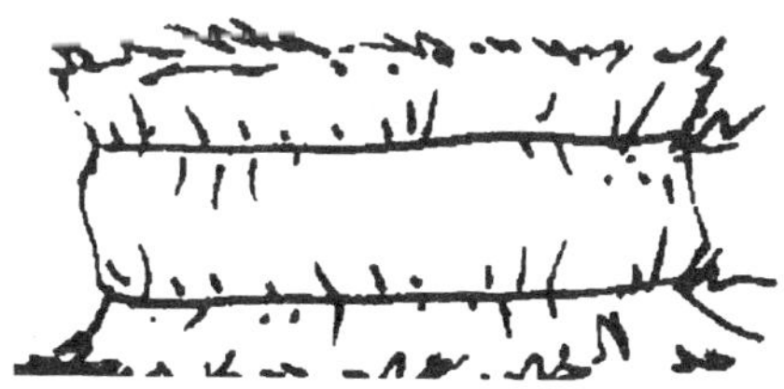

I was feeling a bit silly and numb, and kind of think my judgment may have become a little impaired. I made a quick stop at a "prairie outhouse" but had forgotten how angry a cow can become when she thinks her calf is in danger.

A range cow essentially goes mad when her calf is in danger. She will attack horses, men, wolves, coyotes, snakes, barbed wire fences, bulls, fires, anything. One of the dangers cowboys face is in trying to rescue an injured or sick calf. He'd better have a little talk with the mother first. When you come down to it, a range cow is little more than a wild animal, especially where her young'uns are concerned.

About my encounter in just such a situation, I want to add only one thing. I can testify to the truth of that old saying, "It's definitely much harder for a man to run with his pants down than it is for a woman with her skirt up!"

* * *

We were day-dreamin' about Saturday night, so we just sort of just moseyed around until mid-afternoon. We had rounded up a few additional yearlings, and figured we'd worked long enough.

We thought we'd get back to the corral early, scrape the cow plop off our boots, have nice baths in the stock tank before the rest of the guys got back, the older guys would maybe shave and we'd look slicked up for the ladies when they arrived with dinner.

We'd be leaving early Saturday for town and have lunch there. When we reached the corral we were the last ones in. The stock tank—where all men are equal, more or less—was already full of dirty cowboys.

Foiled again!

#

EPISODE NINETEEN

That waitress saved my life
and helped me regain my cool

Throat on Fire

The round-up was over. The reason we were going to town and do a little celebrating was because branding would be starting on Monday and that was the toughest part of the job. Besides, everybody just felt like kickin' up their heels.

About ten-thirty or eleven Saturday morning our group started drifting into town, the men in their best boots and Stetsons and the women in their prettiest print dresses, and some brought their kids. For the life of me, though, I can't remember which town it was. Don's ranch was about equidistant from Fort Sumner, Vaughn and Roswell.

However, I didn't see Richard Herring again, so it must not have been Fort Sumner. We met at a certain cafe and when everyone was there, we went in and were seated together.

In those depression days throughout the Southwest when you went into a cafe at lunch time, one thing happened with such regularity that it was automatic. You ordered chili and crackers. Everybody did it. I did it in Texas. I did it here. It was the customary thing to do. Chili was hot, it was nourishing, it tasted good, it stuck to your ribs...and it was cheap.

Was that ever a mistake! I hadn't tried New Mexico chili before, and after about the third spoonful I was on fire. It was coursing down my gullet and through my veins like a raging prairie fire.

My eyes and nose were running, I was coughing and nearly gagging, and I could feel the sweat in my hair, on my face and beginning to soak through my clothes. They could see I was in agony. One of those lame-brained practical jokers held up a green pepper and yelled, "Hey, Kid. Eat one of these New Mexico peppers. It'll take the fire right out of that chili."

Everybody else chimed in, "Yeah, Kid, eat some of them peppers. They'll fix it, that's what we do." In desperation, I grabbed the pepper and crammed it into my mouth. My God! It felt like a hot branding iron in my mouth and throat, as if my body was going to burst from pain, and I couldn't get my breath.

I drank all the water within reach and that made it worse. That bunch of crazy waddies was almost hysterical with laughter—wives and kids, too—while by now I'm bathed in sweat and hoping death will come quickly.

The waitress—I swore I'd marry her some day—brought me a heaping bowl of ice cream, then another, and another, giving my "friends" frosty looks that would freeze a rattler. Later on, I did admit that after eating that pepper I sure enough couldn't taste the fire in the chili anymore. And the ice cream was free.

#

EPISODE TWENTY

Real Texans don't buy boots
with walking heels.
If God had intended for man to walk,
He wouldn't have made horses.

Lustin' fer Boots

After lunch we went our separate ways but would all meet later for the Saturday Western Matinee at the movies. I bought some shoe laces and tobacco and found a bench in the shade on the wooden porch of a store front.

I sat there nursing my blistered mouth and throat, putting the laces in my shoes, rolling cigarettes and smoking, watching the people walk by and doing some heavy thinking.

You know, ranch life is so active and consumes so much of every day, there's little time left for thinking. It occurred to me that maybe that is one of the reasons there still were ranchers.

They had just never had the time, or slowed down long enough to take the time, to stop and reflect on the future of what

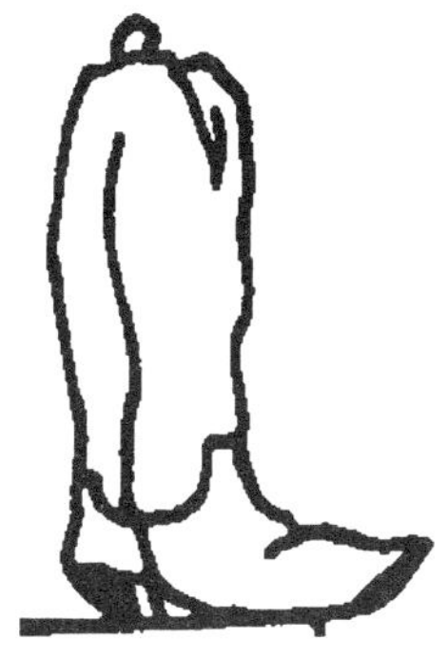

they were doing. And yet, ranching is such a difficult and harsh life their idea that, "Most people are about as happy as they've made up their minds to be," probably helped them to survive those bad times.

It also was proud and honest work, they weren't on the dole, and they did have some fun and the greatest of friends and neighbors.

Then while cogitating, I considered my oxfords. I'd kind of gotten used to wearing women's pants, even if they didn't have any pockets. At least, these buttoned down the front, albeit backwards, instead of down the sides. But those oxfords were an embarrassment. New laces made them feel better but they looked awful, and out of place.

Those bright, shiny, fancy boots walking past looked as pretty as a red heifer in a flowerbed. Lordy, how I lusted for a pair of boots. Almost everybody else in New Mexico wore boots, or at least high-top work shoes. But I had to wear oxfords. I resolved right there, sitting on that bench in New Mexico, watching the pretty girls sashay by, that if I could ever afford it, someday I would wear fine boots, too. Here's what actually happened to that almost sacred promise to myself:

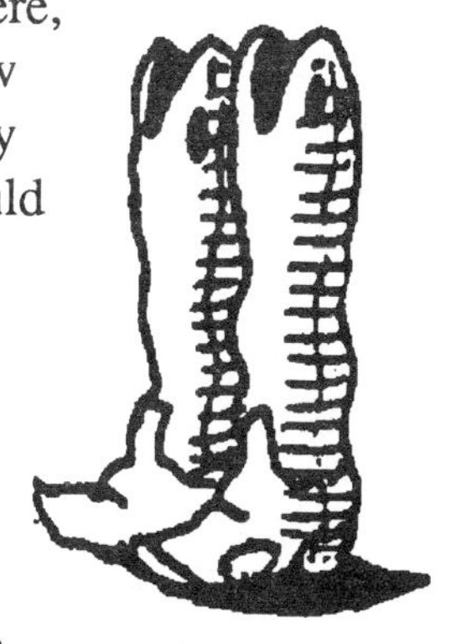

Many years went by and I could finally afford cowboy boots, but I had developed an unstable lower back from a much earlier incident with a bull, and the back doctor had a flat, "No way!" about wearing boots. I'd also gotten bone spurs on one foot, which caused calluses requiring surgical removal two or three times a year.

Although the foot doctor also said, "No way," I still had this burnin' yearnin' to wear boots, and at every opportunity I stopped to gaze wistfully through the windows of boot stores. I was often tempted to go inside, but never did so until urged by my beautiful new bride, Wilsie.

By then I was nearly 75 years old. The salesman, an old cowboy, said, "Those doctors are crazy. Let me tell you why."

The old cowboy salesman continued telling us why boots were so superior to shoes for people with marginal backs and feet, and how now-a-days doctors were prescribing them for those conditions. Meanwhile, he was moving to the shelf and selecting a pair of Lucchese ostrich bellies and slipping them onto my feet.

Wilsie, who wears boots, too, part of the time, was encouraging both of us. For the record, I haven't worn a pair of shoes since, I've not had another back spasm and I've forgotten the foot doctor's name.

"Born to wear boots," my nephew, Jim, says.

#

EPISODE TWENTY-0NE

Rage is fer beasts, not fer men.
It kin burn more'n yer soul

That's a Lot of Bull

This next episode is about that much earlier incident with a bull that caused the lower back pain. It happened at the dairy in Littlefield. Earl was his name. He was a registered, blooded Guernsey. It was his job to keep some 50 milk cows satisfied, happy and productive. He took his job seriously and was very good at it. You might say he took a real delight in his work and was very jealous of it.

For awhile he was kept in a separate pen and his guests would be admitted singly, but old Earl got so mean he started attacking his handlers. They thought letting him out to roam with the cows would improve his disposition, and it did substantially.

But on those days that every cow complained of a headache, old Earl would turn mean again, bellowing, pawing the dirt, shaking his head, just looking for trouble. On such a day I took a load of feed into the field.

Old Earl was really in a frenzy. I got out to close the gate and he got between me and the truck, head down, pawing, bellowing, with blood on his mind. My blood!

A potentially catastrophic situation! I picked up a 2x4 lying by my foot. I had heard that when bulls charge they close their eyes, so here was the game plan: If he charges me, just as he closes his eyes I'll stun him with that 2x4, step aside and let him pass, then run for the truck.

Earl didn't cooperate! He never closed his eyes. When he was almost upon me I swung the 2x4 as hard as I could. It shattered in my hands. It was rotten. His head hit my chest and he took me down, still charging, shoving me along the ground on my back. My arms were pinned underneath and I couldn't reach the ring in his nose.

I stopped sliding and rolled up somersault-style with my hip pockets under his chest and his head in my face, massaging it with his nubbin horns. When he lowered himself to his front knees all that weight on my doubled-over back made my spine start popping and crackling like crazy. That old booger was trying to break my back.

I guy in the barn heard all the commotion Earl was making and came running out with a pitchfork. Jabbing old Earl just made him madder and louder and massage my face with even more vigor. The guy threw down the pitchfork and ran back and got a pale of boiling water.

He threw the whole pale on Earl's main reason for living, scalding that bulbous mass something awful. Earl took off, screaming and moaning and bellowing and kicking his hind legs like the devil himself was after him. My only consolation was that it probably wouldn't matter to Earl for a few days whether his lady friends had headaches or not.

#

EPISODE TWENTY-TWO

Strangers are less so in the West

Hollywood Cowboys

As the people continued coursing past my bench they were beginning to bunch in front of the movie house. Most of my folks were there, too, so I went on over. It was to be a rip-roarin' western, with a newsreel, continued serial and comedy. We'd be busy into the evening.

I loved westerns as a kid and still do. They used to have free movies for us kids on Saturday afternoons in an old store building at Kress, which was an incentive for farmers and ranchers to come in and shop. They were silent movies but I loved such stalwarts of the time as Tom Mix, Ken Maynard, Hoot Gibson and others.

I thought it curious that these certified, dyed-in- the-wool, honest-to-God New Mexico ranch people who were living the western experience would love westerns as much as I did. I mean, considering the fairly obvious fakery involved in scripts and scenes, it would have seemed more logical to me had they been poking fun and laughing at some of the utterly illogical situations on the screen.

That wasn't the case at all. They were consumed with interest and excitement and probably were as appreciative as any audience that had ever seen that movie. I was a little awed by their reaction and later questioned some of them, trying to learn more.

With the Great Depression, the bottom fell out of the beef market, cutting many cowboys and ranchers adrift. At the same time, western movies were doing unusually well, so there was a migration of sorts to Hollywood.

Most of the stars and nearly all of the bit and crowd players had come directly off western ranches and out of the rodeo circuits. These were their people, their friends and relatives, their own kind.

In truth, they were seeing beyond the movie and seeing the faces of the people they cared about. They knew that a casting director could round up 200 cowboys in two days and they didn't feet good about that.

Yet, they were glad some kind of job was out there for the lucky ones and they reacted like they were at a cowboy convention; quite vocal when the bad guys were attacking, or the hero was after a crooked gambler or when he was too shy when the beautiful (and rich) heroine was making up to him.

In 1938 my first wife, Vivian, and I moved from Texas to Los Angeles and after a series of temporary jobs I became a bus driver. The routes were more the interurban type than for street traffic and the two I enjoyed driving the most were to movie studios.

One route went southwest to MGM studios in Culver City, the other went northeast to United Artists, Columbia and Disney, and another in Burbank. We shared the Hollywood bus terminal with Greyhound.

Most of my riders were movie people, including lots of the cowboys who had drifted west. When they found I spoke their kind of lingo it was like getting together with home folks every trip.

Just off Hollywood Boulevard there was a little side street named Gower, about three blocks from the bus terminal. It was where most of the cowboys hung out, dressed in their boots, chaps and hats, waiting for a casting call or studio bus.

It had become known all over town as "Gower Gulch" and had taken on the flavor and character of a small ranching town.

There were bars with swinging doors, domino parlors, barber shops, western movies and sidewalk benches. Sometimes between shifts I'd just walk down there and sit and visit and spin tales for awhile. Salt of the earth, those people. I loved them.

We seldom got top movie stars on the bus, but we did have one, and she was working regularly and riding frequently out to MGM. My favorite female movie star of all time, she was the irrepressible, droll, everybody-was-her-friend, Marjorie Main.

She didn't have to ride the bus, but she loved the studio crowd that usually rode when she did. She'd yell, "Hi Ya, Skip," as she stepped up on board, and then greet everyone else in like manner.

It was party time until she got off, and it was a love affair between her and the cowboys. She was the same person, on and off screen.

#

EPISODE TWENTY-THREE

A lot of journalists have fertilized
the wild-and-wooly reputation of cow country.
But I tell ya, this part of the old West
was no place for amateurs.

Billy the Kid's Grave

Meantime, it was still a Saturday night at the start of the '30s back in Vaughn, New Mexico. Dinner was over, the sun was slipping behind the heat haze, and my friends were looking for action. Temporary baby keepers had been found for the youngsters, and folks were fanning out to the hot spots.

That accounted for everyone but me. Too old for a baby sitter and too young for adult entertainment—although I admit that I did peek inside a few places.

And they WERE having fun, despite the fact that almost anything that was fun, at that time in Vaughn , New Mexico, was also illegal, even for adults. But on balance, apparently the law came down on the side of money being spent and fun being had rather than trying to lock up a bunch of friendly cow people for the night and make them mad enough to swallow a horned toad backwards.

While the night was wearing down I wasn't in on very much that was going on in Vaughn, except randomly, so I'd like to depart from that story a few minutes while telling you about a trip Wilsie and I made to the Fort Sumner area on June 27 and 28, 1996. I'll sprinkle in a few more Vaughan incidents so you can keep up with events of that night while I'm telling you about the trip.

We were hoping to spend two days rummaging around Fort Sumner for any historical data about the people and places important to this story. We stopped en route at Clovis.

It was raining. We had lunch and rented a room. It was still raining. We drove the 90 miles almost to Fort Sumner in the rain. We stopped at the Old Fort Sumner Museum and the adjacent New Mexico State Monument, which are located seven miles southeast of the town of Fort Sumner on Billy the Kid Road, within yards of the banks of the Pecos River.

It still was raining as we visited the museum and Billy's grave, but their rest rooms were the portable type and way out back in the rain, bushes and mud. Of course, we'd been driving in the rain a couple of hours, which didn't help, so we sought and found inside plumbing at the State Monument.

It still was raining and growing too late, so we headed back for Clovis without going downtown, thinking we'd come back the next day before returning home. Wouldn't you know, it rained all that night.

The next morning weather predictions were, "Another rainy day like yesterday," so after breakfast we just headed back home. However, we did pick up some information we think you will find interesting.

I hadn't seen Billy the Kid's gravesite since more than 65 years ago when my friend, Richard Herring, took me there. It only had the tiny granite marker then, later shown on a postcard at the front of the cage, and was hard to find in the undergrowth.

The cage wasn't there then, and neither were the large marker, the pretty wall (I think it had a barbed wire fence then) nor the museum, nor Billy the Kid Road, which leads to it from the highway. At least if the road was there it wasn't marked.

The little headstone has been stolen and recovered twice, once somewhere in Texas. Now, it is not only inside the cage, it is secured in place with strap iron. There are three names on the marker, Billy the Kid across the top; underneath to the left, Tom O'Folliard; and to the right, Charlie Bowdrie. They were buried next to each other. The inscription on the tombstone reads "Truth and history, 21 (indentations like notches on a gun butt) men. Billy the Kid born Nov. 23, 1860...died July 14, 1881. The boy bandit king. He died as he lived."

The following bit of history, replete with abominable spelling, punctuation, grammar, factual errors and flight of flowery imagination, is from the Santa Fe Weekly Democrat of July 21, 1881:

OBITUARY

With His Boots Off

Billy Bonney, alias Antrim, alias Billy the Kid, a twenty-one year old desperado, who is known to have killed sixteen men, and who boasted that he had killed a man for every year of his life, will no more take deliberate aim at his fellow man and kill him, just to keep himself in

> practice. He is dead: and he died so suddenly that he did not have time to be interviewed by a preacher, or to sing hymns, or to pray, before that vital spark had flown, so we cannot say positively that he has clum the shining ladder and entered the pearly gates.
>
> The bullet that struck him left a pistol in the hands of Pat Garrett, at Fort Sumner, last Saturday morning, about half-past 12 a.m. in the room of Pete Maxwell. Governor Lew Wallace will now breathe easier, as well as many others whom he has threatened to shoot on sight.
>
> No sooner had the floor caught the descending form, which had a pistol in one hand and a knife in the other, then there was a strong odor of brim-stone in the air, and a dark figure, with the wings of a dragon, claws like a tiger, eyes like balls of fire, and horns like a bison, hovered over the corpse for a moment, and with a fiendish laugh, said, "Ha! Ha! This is my meat!" and then sailed off through the window. He did not leave his card, but he is a gentlemen well known to us by reputation, and thereby hangs a "tail".

The cemetery, museum and the rather new-looking State Monument are all on the site of the original fort, which had been sold to a fellow named Maxwell at the end of the civil war. The cemetery and the museum properties are now privately owned, as is another museum in downtown Fort Sumner.

We were able to read, but not get copies of, a number of letters written by Billy to Governor Lew Wallace, and from Pat Garrett to his wife. By the way, this was the same Lew Wallace who wrote the famous book, "Ben Hur," while in New Mexico.

The State Monument, officially Fort Sumner State Monument, is dedicated, we were told by the monument manager, Gregory Scott Smith, as a three-part memorial. The memorial is to the Fort Sumner Military Post on whose grounds it stood, to the thousands of Indians who lost their lives through deprivation and brutality, and to the history of Billy the Kid, who was shot and killed there by Sheriff Pat Garrett.

Some people still think of it as an ambush, although Billy was a wanted man.

All remnants of the old fort building are gone, but the park has built waist-high walls, laying out where the building stood and identifying the rooms with what took place there, i.e., where the Maxwells lived, where Pat Garrett shot Billy, where Garrett's henchmen were hiding, and so on.

A lot closer to our home in Amarillo is another spot of history I had visited several times. It also has direct ties to Billy the Kid. This wind-and-sand-swept corner of the world back in the shoot-em-up days really was a bad place.

Bandit gangs were everywhere, and seeming to get away with raping, killing, pillaging. Billy the Kid was among the gangs involved in rustling.

The gravestone name of O'Folliard pops up here, for he, Billy and three other evil types had stolen a small herd of horses from a ranch and drove them to Tascosa, where they stayed until the following winter. Bowdrie—the third name on the gravestone—had remained behind with another gang member in Fort Sumner.

Tascosa is on the north bank of the Canadian River, about 30 miles northward from Amarillo. It is the present site of Cal

Farley's Boys Ranch. Tascosa, for some reason, was abandoned by its residents in the early part of this century. At about the same time I was ridin' the range, Cal Farley wanted to establish a place for wayward or homeless boys. Farley was a former professional wrestler and Amarillo businessman.

The abandoned town of Tascosa and several hundred acres were deeded over to Farley by the then-owner. Original Tascosa buildings that could be salvaged were used by staff and kids until modern facilities could be put in place.

Original land holdings have expanded into thousands of acres, and it has become one of the most successful, privately funded operations of its type in the country, with its Boys Ranch, Girls Home and other youth activities.

Cal Farley and his wife and dog are buried in the original Tascosa cemetery. One of the larger Tascosa buildings, I think the courthouse, has been converted to a historical museum , and there's lots of interesting stuff in there. But, of course, when I visited it several times, I had no special bones to pick, it was just curiosity.

#

EPISODE TWENTY-FOUR

It takes six cups o' town coffee
to equal one cup o' cowboy coffee

Coffee with Personality

Back in Vaughn, New Mexico, it was still a Saturday night in the early '30s, but it was getting late and the high living was beginning to take its toll on my friends in a very visible and vocal manner. They managed to get the kids rounded up and piled into various vehicles and start back home. I was unsure whether the right kids were paired off with the right parents, but no one else seemed to care, so I let it go.

They decided since I was the sober one, another single guy (not so sober) and I should go back out to the corral and spell Don's cowboys so they could go back to the ranch and rest over Sunday. One car swung (that's understated, I'm sure) by the corral and let us off and picked up the other guys and headed on out.

So, we decided that one of us would hit the bedroll while the other kept the cattle together, and take four-hour turns. We flipped and I won first duty in the bedroll. My uncertain buddy managed to saddle and get aboard his horse and wander off among the yearlings, calves and their moms, while I hit the sack.

I awoke the next morning with the sun staring in my face. Startled, I jumped up and looked around. The cattle had scattered to the winds and my friend's horse was standing there asleep, with my friend still in the saddle, also asleep.

I yelled at my hung-over buddy and woke him up and he took off like a shot. I built a fire under the coffee pot, saddled my horse and rode out to help. It turned out not to be a major problem. It was a hot day, the cattle were drowsy, they had grazed well, and most of them were ready to lie down and belch awhile.

As we got ahead of them and were moving them back to the corral, some of the ranchers started drifting back and gave us a hand. We figured if any stragglers were hiding, Don could probably live without them, anyway. When we got back to the corral the coffee had boiled down pretty good, the cook had returned and had steaks and biscuits cooking. My buddy and I were hungry, not having eaten all day. The coffee was pretty pungent, but normal for what cowboys make for themselves, and they liked it.

I've been meaning to tell you about cowboy coffee, and since we're going to be in camp a few days while branding, this is a good time. It is definitely a different experience in coffee. Strong and thick, it smells and tastes very much like the burning hair and hide from a branding iron.

When chewin' that coffee, keep remindin' yourself, it if tastes like mud, it's cause it was ground this morning.

The cook used a big old upright tin pot, the kind you make boiled coffee in, and it held either three or five gallons. The cook built a fire and got that thing boiling way before daylight with what looked like a five-pound bag of coffee grounds.

Since everyone was working in camp and drinking lots of coffee, before lunch and dinner times he added more water and another bag of coffee to the pot. By evening it could walk alone. Today, the raised-pinkie crowd in downtown Portland or San Francisco might pay $5 for coffee just like that if it was served in a demitasse instead of a tin cup.

With the men in camp, the women changed their food routine, bringing lunch instead of the evening meal. It consisted mainly of sandwiches and food that could be held in the hands, because men kept the branding going and spelled each other long enough to grab some food and wolf it down with cups of boiling coffee.

The cook made breakfast and dinner—always biscuits, steak, and onions and potatoes chopped and fried together. A salty sense of humor has to be the best seasoning for range cookin', 'cause most range cooks were worn-out old cowboys too gimpy to work cattle.

And we always had coffee! Of one thing I'm grateful; Styrofoam cups and plates, and plastic knives, forks and spoons, had not been invented then.

#

EPISODE TWENTY-FIVE

Don't approach a horse from the rear,
a bull from the front
or a fool from any direction.

Brandin' Problems

A number of things take place during a branding, none of them happy for the calf, and not especially delightful for the cowboys, either. What I'm doing here is giving you a precautionary note, similar to today's movies—"Scenes depicted herein may contain bloodshed or violence. Parental guidance may be required," or something to that effect.

First, it's helpful to understand that "calf fries" come from somewhere, you don't pick them like strawberries and, second, if you tend to be a little queasy maybe you should consider skipping the next few pages. You can wait for us up ahead.

For a branding, on a large ranch especially, here's the drill: There's about a jillion calves, some with their moms, and yearlings milling around outside the corral gate and being contained by riders. There's a rider at the gate, also, and inside the corral there are more riders, maybe a dozen, and about another dozen men on foot.

We're running two lines, so there are two fires heating branding and cauterizing irons. The coffee pot is over its own fire near the fence, so it doesn't get kicked over and scald someone.

Crutch, Roy, Jack and Don were among the inside riders; the first three because they were the best ropers, and they needed to teach me what to do; and Don, whether sober or not, because these were his calves. He had final call if anything unusual came up. Me, I was on the ground.

I was a "flanker" and hind-leg man on one team. There was also a front-leg man, then a guy who used the branding and cauterizing irons and kept them hot, and the swabs, another fellow with a very sharp and clever knife, and yet another guy that gave the calves shots and looked them over to check their health.

How does one flank a calf? You face its left side, your right hand grasping its right flank, your left hand under its neck, and you yank upward hard as you can at the same time kind of falling backward, pulling the calf over your bent knees and onto the ground on its left side.

Quickly, you slide around behind the calf, engaging his lower leg with your foot and pressing forward while grabbing his upper leg and pulling backward. Your partner grabs the upper front leg and bends the knee, while pressing down on the calf with his own knee. If you do it correctly, the calf is immobilized with its working parts exposed.

Now, try that on a 500-pound yearling! That's what we had

to do. Maybe a fourth of that herd had been missed in the last branding. Ideally, the riders would rope the right hind leg of yearlings and drag them up to you already down. Then, all you had to do was quickly jump into your positions, slip the rope off and hold on.

But Jack was the only one who could do that consistently. Heck, Jack even brought us the calves that way. What a great roper he was. The other riders felt lucky to get a rope around their necks.

I suspect you may be asking yourself about what was happening to Ora Lee's pants that I was wearing. Well, thoughtfully, Crutch brought an old pair of leather chaps for me to wear, which did the job.

Oh, there's one other thing for the back-leg guy to remember. If you don't want poop all over you, you'd better hold the calf's tail down.

Inside riders bring calves into the corral in groups of 20 or 30, rope them individually and drag them to one of the ground teams. They try not to let the calf's mother in, because she will usually create all kinds of havoc when she sees her young'un being manhandled and hears it bawling.

She'll charge men on the ground, run through branding-iron fires, anything to protect her calf. Jack's alert rope saved us several times. He could take a cow down and hog-tie her quicker than it takes to tell about it.

#

EPISODE TWENTY-SIX

Warning: This ain't parlor talk

Bucket Full of What?

The team works quickly. The fellow with the hot branding iron presses it against the calf's hair and hide until they're sizzling, while the knife guy, if it's a heifer, cuts a distinctive notch in her ear, and if it's a bull, also castrates it. The branding-iron fellow comes back with a red-hot cauterizing iron and cauterizes the castration wound. Another guy is standing ready with a swab from a bucket of hot tar and creosote and swabs out the cavity and cauterized area.

This is done to prevent flies and later, maggots, from attacking the affected area. If that happens, the calf may die.

I don't believe any man likes to do that operation, even seasoned old cowpunchers who've done it most of their lives. They can't help relating to the calf personally. I knew about it, of course; that's an essential part of raising beef, but didn't like it and felt sick about it. Still, if I wanted to be a cowboy I had to do what I had to do.

But even in bad situations humorous things happen. The wives were there with lunch, in a group sitting or leaning along the corral fence. The men started eating, spelling each other while the work went on. I was at the fence with the ladies, having a sandwich when one of Don's cowboys, the one with the knife, very bashfully approached Don's wife:

"Ma'am" he said, "Don sent me over to see you. We need a bucket."

(Remember, this was her first branding, too.)

"Whatever for?" she asked. He kept looking at the ground, some of the women started snickering.

"Well, Ma'am, becuz the other bucket's full," he finally blurted out.

"Full of what?" she demanded.

By now his face was beet colored. Don's wife was growing irritated and the other women are howling.

"Thaings," he said, still looking down.
"You know, those little thaings you get at brandings."

Don's wife was beginning to think she was being made the butt of a joke and she was getting angry.

"Cowboy, tell me what you're talking about this minute," she demanded.

"Ah jes can't do that, Ma'am," he said softly and walked away.

A couple of the ladies explained to Don's wife what the "thaings" were and what the bucket was for. She turned crimson and clasped her hand over her mouth in embarrassment. She went to the truck and got a bucket. I took it to the cowboy for her. I'd finished my sandwich, anyway, and was struggling with a cup of coffee.

People have asked whether the camp cook served calf fries, or Rocky Mountain Oysters, as they were called then, for dinner. The answer is an emphatic, No! Nobody would have eaten them. I've never tasted them. I've never known a working cowboy who has or would. But some city folks seem to think they are a delicacy. That's what the buckets were for; someone was running them into town and selling them.

In a way, it was hard to break camp, say goodbye and head back to our respective ranches. We'd worked hard, gotten a lot done, pulled a lot of stunts on each other and shared a lot of bad coffee. But it had been very satisfying. Now it was time to go.

I mentioned to Roy, as we were riding our horses back to his ranch, that several of the cowboys had told me they were riding a "Roy Skipworth horse." It was spoken with pride, like a man might say he's driving his Packard, or a woman casually mentioning her Dooney-Bourke purse. Of course, they meant a horse Roy had broken and trained, which I already knew a little something about, but I asked him anyway: What made his horses so special?

Roy believed there were two ways of doing it. You can break and train a horse using kindness and patience to gain its trust and respect, so that it thinks of the rider as a leader and friend. It wants to work and cooperate with him. Horses enjoy working in that situation. But the process takes a long time. Roy said he had lots of time and lots of patience and liked the friendship and loyalty his horses developed. He never used cruelty or hurt a horse. He rarely used spurs and then only little short nubbins.

Too many men, Roy felt, try to break horses using cruelty and fear to motivate, and I saw some of that, too. These were men who use quirts or ropes to try to whip horses into submission, spade bits that dig into the tongue when reins are yanked, and star spurs that draw blood with each rake of the flanks. There also were those who penned up broncs without food or water until they were too weak to resist. The ranching community frowned on these practices and was trying its best to get them outlawed. Those horses would wind up mean, afraid and cantankerous. They were non-responsive and would dump, kick or bite their riders or run away at any opportunity.

It is my understanding that today's ranchers are a lot more humane in their treatment of livestock. That branding and ear-notching, for instance, has been replaced by ear-tags, and those spade bits and star-spurs and other implements of torture may be illegal.

* * *

It has been said that if a man leaves his ranch for a couple of weeks everything that can go wrong has gone wrong. Of course, Roy's precious broncs in the corral were waiting. Ora Lee and the kids had seen to it they had plenty of feed and water and were OK but other things, well, it seems like if you're not watching, they fall down. Like the outhouse!

Despite all that, and there was lots to do, I kept thinking how great it was going to be to have a real bath that night—carrying water and all—and sleep in a real bed not infested with imaginary rattlesnakes. You just can't sleep well with one eye open.

Roy kept worrying about the nesters. He felt a real concern and responsibility for their well-being, and suggested that maybe right after breakfast in the morning I'd better take a ride up there. He asked Ora Lee to fix a bag of food staples and a slab of bacon for me to take along. The truth is, I was uneasy about the nesters, too, and happy for the chance to go back. They were such nice people.

#

EPISODE TWENTY-SEVEN

Close friends are folks
who've sopped gravy
outa the same skillet.

Big Hearts 'n Nothin' Else

About dawn the next morning I mounted up, a gunny sack of food hanging from the saddle horn, and set out for the nesters. There is something very satisfying to the soul being astride your favorite horse and alone, enjoying the wonders of nature. Most cowboys feel it's about as close to God as they'll ever get.

Upon reaching their place I had a surprise coming. This family had "adopted" another nester family and set them up in what once had been a barn, and they were all working toward improving living conditions, apparently giving first priority to comfort facilities.

(Editor's note—"Comfort facilities" is Skip's euphemism for what is otherwise known in the west as an outhouse, a Chic Sale, one-holer, thunder station, Sears catalog dispensary or The American.)

The first family greeted me like a long-lost son, quietly but with such expressive eyes. They introduced me to all the members of the new family as if I was some kind of saint, amid howdying, shaking hands and back-slapping. I felt embarrassed. After all, I was only the messenger, but that cut no ice with them. I was one of their own.

I took the sack of provisions (that Ora Lee had fixed) down from the saddle and spread it out on a bench. Silent tears started rolling down faces of the adults. As the adults hugged me the kids were reaching for my hands and pants legs, whatever they could touch. It was a scene frozen in my memory; these proud people, so good, so down to earth, yet with so little hope for the future. I wondered, is this the true meaning of God's Spirit?

It was so typical of rural families in the Great Southwest. Here was the first family, living in old abandoned ranch shacks with almost nothing, taking in a second family who had even less, and doing it with outstretched arms. It's still like that today in this part of the country. It seems like people with the least are the very first to offer help. And they mean it.

Someone scared up a cup of hot coffee for me and a piece of hardtack, and the adults and I sat and talked awhile. Both families had operated small farms and ranches in the Texas Panhandle, although they hadn't know each other at the time, and had almost identical experiences. They had small mortgages with their banks, the banks failed, wiping out their savings, and they were in default when they couldn't pay off the mortgage.

A Wall Streeter named Hickman Price, heading a group of New York investors, bought their mortgages for cents on the dollar, along with hundreds of other mortgages, foreclosed and served eviction notices. These families, like many others, loaded what possessions they could on whatever vehicles they had and watched as the new owner's tractors pushed down what had been their homes, windmills, barns, haystacks, whatever else was standing, and burned them in order to clear the grounds for huge farming operations.

Collectively, perhaps a hundred or more small farms and ranches in that area, and thousands of acres, were involved in what was considered to be a huge land grab by Hickman Price. Many thought it illegal, many begged for government intervention, but to no avail.

(I might add that about three years later Price and his group went bankrupt themselves, after losing thousands of acres of wheat to "mysterious" fires, in the area generally known as "Nance Ranch." Price's farm machinery covered about 20 acres near downtown Kress and it was sold to the highest bidders...for cents on the dollar.)

There were thousands of families in similar situations, destitute, their remaining possessions in their vehicles. They were from Texas, Oklahoma, Nebraska, roaming the highways and byways generally westward, looking for roofs over their heads and food for their children. I reminded my friends that Roy said they could slaughter a beef when they needed to, and to come up to the ranch house if they were in need, or in case of illness or accident. I also warned about rattlesnakes and scorpions lurking about those old buildings.

Luckily, for bathing purposes there still was a working windmill there, although people couldn't drink the gyppy water. A small creek nearby, with water "too thin to plow, too thick to drink," provided their drinking water. They assured me they were boiling it long and hard before drinking it or making coffee.

Leave-taking was hard, even harder than the first time because I had the feeling this might be the last time that I'd see them , which turned out to be true. I've often wondered about them.

When my horse and I got out of sight, we stopped for a little while to enjoy the scenery and think about things. I don't know what my horse thought about but my mind was on the nesters. What would happen to them?

By the way, don't ever confuse the term "nesters" with "squatters," the latter being one of the scourges of the old West. Squatters came with fence posts, barbed wire, sometimes sheep, and the intention of permanently homesteading on land owned by others, without right, title or payment of rent.

Back on my horse and heading for home, over the next hill I could see someone waving a tablecloth from the windmill tower. I waved my floppy hat back and headed on in. That used to be the universal signal meaning, "Come to the house."

Roy and Crutch were standing in the yard, talking. Roy told me that Jack was going to be appearing in a rodeo for a few days, and Crutch needed me to help him while Jack was gone. If it was OK with me, I was to unsaddle my horse and get my things together. We'd be leaving right away.

#

EPISODE TWENTY-EIGHT

A bronc rider should be light in the head
and heavy in the seat.

If you ain't got a choice, be brave.

The Practical Joke

Crutch, being several years older than Roy, was beginning to show the effects of ranch life in his stiff movements and gimpy walk, and the lines were deeper in his face. But he and Roy both were still very handsome men.

Crutch had a roguish look about him, a devil-may-care attitude and always a twinkle in his eye, as if planning a huge practical joke. He and Jack were by far the worst offenders in a world of practical jokers. And I happen to hate practical jokes.

As we approached his ranch it was with some trepidation that I anticipated being there and working with him. I wanted to be there, I admired the man, perhaps was even a little in awe of him, but this little caution light kept blinking in my mind to be on the lookout for practical jokes. I should have paid closer attention to that blinking light.

The house was large. It had several bunkhouses, giving the impression the ranch was once a good-sized operation. There was a nice stream curling around two sides but no windmill, so apparently the stream flowed year-round. There was a streambed crossing maybe a quarter-mile from the house but the banks were

exceedingly high and steep. Still, it was fordable if you got a good run coming down the far side. Crutch's wife, Maidie, had supper almost ready and Jack was already at the table looking at rodeo brochures.

As I pulled up a chair I was struck by an indescribably awful smell which, after I'd tentatively sniffed everything on my plate, turned out to be the glass of water. They were watching, quizzically, and looking at each other. I'd embarrassed myself and them, too, and I was squirming but not before blurting out, "What's wrong with this awful water?" Crutch said, "Well, it's cistern water and we think maybe its gone a little bad."

During the supper conversation, Crutch asked me if I like bacon for breakfast. Already in trouble, I might as well tell the truth. "I like 'bought' bacon but I sure don't like salt pork," I told him. Crutch allowed rather sharply, "You'll eat salt pork." The caution light started blinking. When they told me Jack would be riding with us the next morning until about noon before leaving for the rodeo, that made the light start blinking again. Was something really afoot or was it just my nerves and suspicious nature?

Jack's quarters were in one of the bunkhouses. They gave me the one next to his. As I moved about unpacking my trumpet case, I was expecting a booby trap but all was peace and quiet that night.

We had breakfast of coffee made with that awful cistern water, biscuits, eggs and, of course, salt pork. Then Crutch gave me a small job to do that would keep me in the house about a half hour. He and Jack would go on to the corral and saddle up the horses and wait for me there.

This smelled like a setup. The caution light was blinking like one, too. But, nevertheless, I completed my assigned task, got my hat and walked toward the corral.

What turned out to be Crutch's and Jack's horses were tied outside the fence. The third horse, my horse, was standing nearby with Crutch facing him and holding on to his bridle. Jack was leaning up against the horse on the left side, helping him maintain his balance. That was because his left hind hoof was hoisted off the ground with a rope tied to the saddle horn. The horse was skittery and nervous, his ears were back and he had a mean look in his eyes.

Any fool knowing Crutch and Jack would recognize this as a setup, and the caution light was no longer blinking, it was a bright, steady amber. Crutch told me to hurry and get in the saddle while they held the horse. I asked if he had been ridden before. They told me sure, lots of times, he was just a little frisky in the mornings. I knew they were lying and I was scared. I wasn't ready for this.

Crutch yelled, "Come on, Kid, Roy said you're a good rider." This was what you would now call the "Defining Moment." If I rode I'd likely get hurt. If I didn't I'd be called "Chicken" and become known as afraid to ride horses.

I couldn't have that happen and still be a ranch hand. In my best swagger I walked over to Jack and said, "C'mon, Pardner, help me up on this nag."

As soon as I got my feet in the stirrups I nodded to Jack and he quickly cut the rope to the saddle horn. The horse stood there about a second. Crutch let out a war whoop and whapped him several times across the face with his hat; old Jack yelled and slapped the horse on his rump.

That horse went crazy, bucking like I never saw before. As he was going up I was coming down. When the horse went down I went up, and you could have driven a pickup between the saddle and seat of my pants.

I lost the reins with the first jump and was pulling leather in all desperation. (That's a no-no in bronc riding, but I wasn't proud by then. I was trying to save my life.)

The horse continued bucking, fishtailing, corkscrewing, first this way and then that way. When he couldn't buck me off he tried to spin me off or hit the ground stiff-legged to jar me off.

After a period of violent maneuvers he took off on a dead run. I took stock of my situation. I was no longer in the saddle. My right leg was all the way down into the coil of rope hanging from the saddle horn; my left leg was straddling the cantle across the back of the saddle; I was holding the horn with my right hand and cantle with my left. Neither foot was in a stirrup. The reigns, knotted, were up around the horse's ears. I couldn't reach them.

He was running like the wind. Faster than I'd ever been on a horse before. It was all I could do to hold on and then I saw he was headed toward a dry draw running across the valley floor. It looked about 10 feet across. I couldn't see the bottom. It didn't help to remember that a horse's vision is not any better than a man's. I couldn't jump off, I was too tangled in rope. As we drew closer would he stop suddenly at the edge, or whirl into a turn? Either would dump me. I needed to brace myself, one way or the other. But he surprised me! Still in a full run, he jumped the draw, never wavering, with me still clinging to the saddle for all my life.

I'd guess it was about five miles later when the horse started slowing to a gallop, obviously getting winded, and finally he slowed to a trot. As he trotted, his head came up and the reins slid down his neck where I could reach them. He had made a semicircle after jumping the draw and was headed back toward it, but further down where it fanned out onto the prairie and was easy to cross. He yielded to the reins as I guided him back toward the corral. I managed to get back into the saddle but with my right leg still snarled in the rope. I swore I'd kill Crutch and Jack with my bare hands.

Both those guys had laughed themselves almost sick, but they very carefully got me untangled and down from the saddle. They were so nice I decided not to kill them, after all. At least for awhile.

Crutch said, "Kid, we lied. That was a wild stallion. He's never been ridden before. And Son, (Notice that? Now I'm Son.) I gotta tell you. It wasn't pretty but that was the damndest ride I ever saw in my life."

Under my breath I said, "Yeah, and the luckiest."

Jack threw his saddlebags on his horse and rode off to the rodeo. Crutch and I unsaddled and went in to lunch. That bit about the three of us riding together had been just part of their nefarious plan.

#

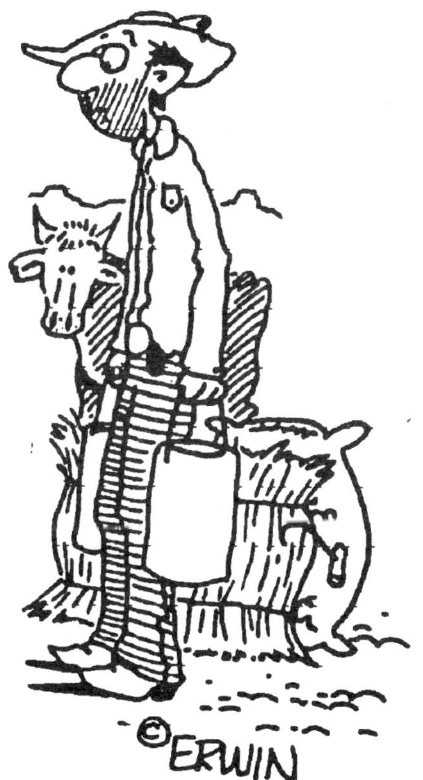

EPISODE TWENTY-NINE

Clean socks in a bunkhouse is
the rarest thing in the West, but
water sometimes can be more whiffy
than a man

CLEANIN' OUT THE CISTERN

At lunch, even Crutch and Maidie complained about the water. It is so hard not to drink while eating, but the odor and taste were enough to gag me. Crutch said he had a long ladder and that after we ate he and I were going to check the cistern.

I suppose most of you know what a cistern is. At that time, rural America was covered with them. Actually, a cistern is nothing more than a hole in the ground—it's usually floored and lined with brick or concrete—which is used to store water. In most cases, it was guttered rainwater runoff from the roof of the house or other buildings, diverted by gutter or pipe into the cistern. That was the case at Crutch's house. Of course, bird droppings, dead insects, dirt or anything else on a roof washed right into the cistern with the rainwater. You're thinking, "How horrible!" and you are right. But at least it was wet. Water, any kind of water, was mighty precious in that country.

We lowered the ladder down into the cistern. Crutch got a lantern and lighted it and I went down to have a look. The stench was bad but what I saw was worse. Decomposed carcasses were floating all over the surface; at least six rabbits, numerous ground squirrels, rats and mice, several rattlesnakes and lizards, some birds, hundreds of bugs and lots of trash.

I went up the ladder and reported to Crutch. We agreed the only thing to do was bail it all out, clean and disinfect the cistern and haul water up from the stream to refill it, at least partially. Never mind that all the ranch cattle, as well as wild animals, drank from the stream, too, and waded in it and no telling what else. I didn't want to think about it.

There was a two-gallon bucket on the cistern rope and a pulley across the top. We had a couple of gallon coffee cans that I used from the ladder steps to bail with. I'd fill the bucket and Crutch would hoist it up and empty it and lower it back down. It was a long, backbreaking job but went smoothly until about two feet from the bottom, where it was almost entirely mud and silt. That was heavy and it was nasty, but I got all I could, scooping the last

few inches with my hands. What we needed now was fresh water to rinse out the rest of the muck and wash it down, and that had to come from the stream. That's when Crutch introduced me to his "water wagon." It was an old '29 Model A Ford roadster with no top...and no brakes. Where the storage space, or optional "rumble seat" would have been in the turtleback area behind the driver's compartment, Crutch had done what many people did in those days—he converted the roadster to a pickup truck—before pickups were invented.

He had taken the lid off the "turtle," made and fitted a wooden platform to fit the floor and hang out the back, bored a hole through the platform and floor, dropped a bolt in the hole so the platform couldn't slide out and he had a quick-change pickup. Crutch had mounted two open 55-gallon steel drums, which stood upright on the platform.

Crutch explained he ordinarily used the vehicle to bring water up from the stream each week so Maidie would have plenty of water to do the laundry. He thought he'd better go with me on the first trip because, as he said, "It's a little tricky getting back up the bank with those barrels of water."

It was the fording point we'd used before and there was ample room to turn around. It was wide and had a rocky bottom, meaning only about three or four inches of water flowing. Filling the barrels took a long, long time, standing on rocks and dipping a little bit in buckets and pouring. But we finally got it done. Getting out was something else.

The vehicle was headed toward home, and under Crutch's coaching this is what we did:

We backed across the stream and up the far bank as fast as we could until the engine stalled, which it did each

time. Then, in rapid order, push in the clutch, pick up speed going back down, shift into low, restart the engine and race up the opposite bank. When the engine stalls, race back up the far bank again. Each time we sloshed out a lot of water, but each time we got a little higher. Finally, after four or five repeats, we pulled out. We got back to the cistern just as it was getting dark.

We kept some of the water for drinking, and by lantern light we used the rest of the water to wash down the cistern, scrub it down and bail it out again. Maidie gave us some old towels to dry it.

#

EPISODE THIRTY

Pickin' up bones to keep from starvin'
Pickin' up chips to keep from freezin'
Pickin ' up courage to keep from leavin'
Way out West in no-man's land.
(Sign on a wagon)

The real Llano Estacado

The next day and for several days following, Crutch was out early working the ranch and was back at sundown, leaving me to refill the cistern. It required lots of dipping of a lot of water and lots of trips to the stream and back but I got it done.

In the meantime, while I'm dippin' 'n pourin' I'll tell you another story. This one's about the plains of Texas, Oklahoma and New Mexico. Some of you have not been so fortunate as to have seen or lived on the plains, the "Llano Estacado." Those of you who have may not realize that centuries ago there may have been people who perhaps shared your observations about this place. It was our aim to find out for you.

Therefore, as a public service to you, Wilsie and I went to the Carson County Square House Museum in Panhandle on Aug. 28, 1996, and after lengthy research found a couple of very interesting documents about these plains. Tell me if you think there's much difference between what they thought then and what you think now.

The first document is attributed to Coronado but actually was found in the journal of Pedro de Cataneda, who was the official historian for Coronado's expedition of 1541. He recorded his observations of the plains:

"Here they saw cows (buffalo) for two days....The country the buffalo traveled over was so level and smooth that if one looked at the cows the sky could be seen between their legs. At a distance they looked like smooth-trunked trees whose tops joined.

"The country was like a bowl so that when a man sat down, the horizon surrounded him all around at a distance of a musket shot. There were no groves of trees except at the rivers, which flowed at the bottom of some ravines. Several lakes were found at intervals; they were round as plates, a stone's throw across.

"The grass grew tall near these lakes; away from them it was short, a span or less. It was impossible to find tracks in this country because the grass straightened up again as soon as it was trodden down. No track was found of where they went and on this account it was necessary to mark the road, by which they went, with cow dung, so as to return."

The second account is by Capt. Randolph B. Marcy, who laid out the Santa Fe Trail, known as the Ridge Route, in 1849. Capt. Marcy wrote in his journal:

"We have passed over a high rolling prairie for the past three days, destitute of wood, except a narrow fringe of trees upon the borders of ravines...a soil worthless and utterly unfit for cultivation. When we were upon the table-land, a view presented itself as boundless as the ocean. Not a tree, a shrub or any other object, either animate or inanimate, relieved the dreary monotony of the prospect. It was a vast, illimitable expanse of desert prairie...the dreaded 'Llano Estacado.' Or in other words, the great Sahara of North America. It is a region almost as vast and trackless as the ocean...a land where no man, either savage or civilized, can permanently abide. It spreads forth into a treeless, desolate waste or uninhabited solitude, which always has been and must continue to be, uninhabited forever; even the savages dare not venture to cross it except at two or three places where they know water can be found...It would seem as if the Creator had designed this as a great natural barrier, beyond which agriculturists should not pass."

(Quotes from Marcy's journal used by permission of Dr. L.F. Sheffy. See Marcy's journal quote from Grant Foreman in "Marcy and the Gold Seekers" on page 17, Sheffy's "Timothy Dwight Hobart.")

We also bought a little booklet titled "Voices of the Square House" by Charles Deahl and illustrated by Floyd Scott, whom we met while there. I don't have permission to copy all of it, but wanted you to read a couple of excerpts and see if they ring a bell. Here's the first:

"If there was one thing that summed up
What it was like to live out here
In this...this...nowhere...
It was the cowchips.
Every time I picked one up I said

Yessir...this is fine...this is just fine...
This is the way a lady should
Spend her time...
She should be out here
Picking up cowchips
To take back to her dugout and warm it
And to cook her family's meal on it.
Yessir...this is just fine..."

* * *

Did you ever pick up any cowchips? Heck, I did. As a kid in the depression. Wagon loads of them. My horses were so well-trained that when I gleaned the last in one area they knew it. They'd just walk on up to the next area and wait for me there. I suppose Providence always provides. My mom also cooked for her family with them ...and warmed the house with them.

The second quote has a lot more truth than anyone would like to admit; something you know for sure in your heart but can't prove:

"I bought a section from Simpson
On the other side of Barstow's ranch from mine.
In the spring of '14 I started across Barstow's
With seventy-three head and got to my new section with thirty-eight.
In November I started out from the new section
With thirty-six head (two fell through the ice in Gleason's pond),
Picked up what I figured were my strays as I crossed Barstow's,
And got back to my place with ninety head.
In '33 while everybody was blowing away
I was living in town and driving a Pierce Arrow."

Let me throw in one more for good measure:

"It might not have been so bad I think,
If it had not been for the hope.
The land was so bare, so absolutely
Without anything already,
That you thought it just had to get better,
To make you better with it.
I wouldn't have minded so much,
I suppose,
If I had not ever hoped things would be so good."

OK, just one more:

"I loved that tree so much
That I got to where I hated
The sight of it or even the thought of it.
I carried water clear out there to it for twenty years
And damned myself every time I did it.
It wouldn't grow but it wouldn't die,
So I could be happy with it
But I couldn't give up on it either."

OK, back to the cistern now. Maidie was so proud to have fresh (well, reasonably so) water for her cooking, dish washing and laundry and for all of us to drink. I think she was a little ill when she looked down the hill from the cistern and saw where Crutch had dumped the stuff we bailed out.

It didn't make me feel too good, either. When Crutch came in for dinner that night he said, "Son, you did real good. That water tastes fine and the cistern is full."

I was glad. It seemed important to me for Crutch and Maidie to be please.

Crutch told me that night to get my bedroll together. The next morning, early, we were driving over to a neighbor's house and borrow a truck and go up into the mountains for a load of wood. We'd be there overnight and come back the next day.

Maidie was almost out of firewood for her cooking and washing and he needed to lay in a supply of stovewood for the winter. If we waited much longer it might be snowing up where he wanted to go and it would be almost impossible to get a truck in and out of there.

#

EPISODE THIRTY-ONE

A rattler in the grass is bad enuf.
One in the bedroll is a mighty unwelcome guest.

Rattler in the Bedroll

It was a '26 or '27 Chevy truck, which at that time was little more than a coupe with larger wheels in the rear and a flat bed, in this case because the owner used it for hauling hay. It had the same little four-cylinder engine and three-speed stick transmission as the passenger car.

Typically, the two-wheel rear brakes had been used up long before. Not too good, I thought, for mountain driving.

Just as the sun came up we piled into the truck and left. We had waited for daylight; we had no lights. We were headed for the Lincoln National Forest in an area we called the Capitan Mountains.

(Note: I guess map nomenclature tends to change. At that time that whole range was known as the White Mountains, and five years later when I was in the Civilian Conservation Corps near Cloudcroft it still was called the White Mountains. Now, the map shows it as the White Mountain Wilderness Area. Maybe you get the drift.)

Considering it was a narrow twisting dirt road up the side of the mountain with lots of ups and downs, and that we had no brakes, Crutch did a masterful job of up-shifting and down-shifting and keeping us on the road. Well into the forested area we came to a small valley with a clearing by the road, the place Crutch was looking for. He backed the truck in and announced this was where we were camping.

Maidie had packed sandwiches for us and Crutch had filled a couple of canvas water bags with that good cistern water so the first thing we did was have a nice leisurely lunch.

People were permitted to pick up all the "downed wood" they wanted. There was a heavy growth of timber around us and Crutch explained the "downed wood" rule, which simply meant the tree had to be dead and no longer upright. A dead tree still standing was not eligible for taking. Crutch also said he wanted wood about the girth of a fence post, reasonably straight, branches trimmed off and six to eight feet long so they could be loaded across the truck bed.

I thought he sounded a bit choosy but, really, when we picked up our axes and went into the woods it was no problem at all to find and trim wood the way he liked. It was about dusk when I dragged the last of my wood for the day to the campsite. Crutch was already there and had built a fire. The coffee was boiling and several generous slices of salt pork were sizzling in a skillet.

Evening chill of the mountain air made the fire feel good, and the coffee, whatever else might be said about it, was steaming hot. I wished then and many times before and since that I could learn to drink hot coffee from a tin cup without burning my lips.

It had been a long tiring day and growing colder with nightfall so we soon crawled into our bedrolls. Mine was close to the remaining coals of the campfire and soon I was warm and sound asleep. It was a very deep sleep and in the shadowy dawn it was hard to cut through the sleep-haze and fully awaken.

I remember the aroma of coffee and salt pork and smoke from the fire, and the dim figure of Crutch standing over my head

holding a boulder the size of a volley ball. He was saying something, barely above a whisper.

"Wake up, Son, but don't move a muscle. Don't even twitch and don't say anything. There's a rattlesnake coiled up by your head. Now, blink your eyes if you understand me."

It flashed through my mind this was another one of his practical jokes and I was angry. I had the urge to reach back and pull his legs out from under him but he began to repeat the warning and I thought I could hear a slight rattling to the right of my head...up close.

I blinked, big. Crutch continued.

"Now, Son, keep still. Keep your eyes on this rock. It is directly above the rattler. When I turn loose you roll to your left as quick and far as you can and I'll jump backward. Watch the rock. NOW!"

The rock dropped, I rolled to the left, Crutch jumped. My bedroll, with me still in it, rolled a full 10 feet. I could hear the rattlesnake thrashing about, its rattlers stirring up a storm. Crutch had broken its back. We finished killing it and Crutch put on some more salt pork to fry as though nothing had happened.

Over breakfast, Crutch told me he'd seen the snake crawl up past my shoulders and coil up, but couldn't tell whether it came from inside the bedroll or along the outside. He said he'd waited about 10 minutes for the snake to settle down. He'd hoped it would crawl away, but it didn't.

Crutch had inched his way to my bedroll with the boulder, as quietly as possible, trying not to awaken either me or the snake. Evidently, the rattler had spent most of the night up against my warm body.

We loaded the wood on the truck, first driving stakes upright into the sideboard stanchions on all four corners of the bed to keep the load from shifting or rolling. The top of the load was about level with the top of the cab and I thought it was a pretty good load.

But Crutch wanted more. So we went back into the woods and brought back about that much again and loaded that on top of the other. That little old truck looked like a tumblebug trying to carry a dung-ball.

We cranked up the engine and tried to climb back up the little valley to the road. The front wheels came off the ground and the engine stalled. We started rolling backward and Crutch put it in reverse and tried to restart the engine. It didn't work and the truck almost did a backward somersault. I jumped out and threw a small log under the back wheels. It almost flipped backward again but it stopped.

Crutch agreed the load was too big. We off-loaded the extra wood we'd loaded that morning and finally got out. We came back the next day and picked it up.

Even carrying those smaller loads down that mountain was a hair-raising experience, the truck being so under-powered, top-heavy, overloaded and without brakes. But Crutch seemed perfectly unaware of hazards that were so obvious to me.

Finally, I mentioned the snake again, thanking Crutch for his quick-thinking and for saving my life. You know, it's almost impossible to do anything about a bite around the face or throat, especially with no anti-venom or other first-aid materials. Crutch said, "Aw, shucks," and expressed the opinion that I would have done it for him.

I pondered that. Would I? Would I have been that clever? Crutch was within inches of the snake when standing over me holding that boulder. He was wearing boots, but an adult snake's fangs can penetrate boot tops. Especially badly worn boots as his were.

Then I told Crutch about being so sure he was pulling a practical joke on me and if I hadn't heard the rattle I'd have yanked his feet out from under him, boulder and all. He said that was his biggest worry. After lying to me about that wild horse he was afraid I wouldn't believe him about the rattler, and that was the trouble with practical jokes. Sometimes they're not jokes at all.

Then Crutch surprised me. Up to then I'd thought him a little aloof toward me.

"Son," he said, "you haven't got a pappy and I feel bad about that. I feel like I need to talk to you like I was your pappy. Is it all right with you and will you listen to me?"

I assured him it was OK and I would listen. As near as I can remember it went like this:

"First off, don't worry about no more practical jokes or hasslin' from me and Jack. There'll be no more of that. When you came here, Roy told me you were aimin' to stay in this country for good and be a cowhand and try to become a rancher. "Well, that's a good aim except there's no place for more cowhands with this depression. We get drifters by here all the time, 40 or 50 years old, no family, so stove up they can't do nothin' except from the back of a horse, wantin' to work for their keep and tobacco. Small ranchers like me and Roy can't even afford that, things are so bad.

"Periodically, we've been gettin' kids like you, except older. Kids belongin' to relatives. Runaways. Well, they're kin. They think they can be cowboys but nobody needs cowboys and we can't run them off because of being kin-folks. So me and Roy have been just working the britches off them and rough-housin' them a little, like we did you, but within a week they'd all high-tailed it out of here."

By now, we had unloaded the second load of wood at Crutch's house and returned the truck to the neighbors, picked up our "water wagon" and were on the way home. But Crutch wasn't through talking to me.

#

EPISODE THIRTY-TWO

The West is a great playground
Fer young men

A Cowboy, Once Upon a Time

Crutch went on, "But you were different. Stubborn I guess. Everything we did you took it and grinned and kept askin' fer more. Hell, by all rights you shoulda skedaddled outa here long ago. You've worn us out tryin' to think of new things for you to tackle. Trouble is, we've come to like you too much now to try to run you off anymore. Me and Roy couldn't pay nothin' but we'd keep you here if we had our way, even if your ropin' does need a little honin'.

“That’s why I’m talkin’ to you like this. Tryin’ to get through that thick head of yours and pound some sense into it. If you really think you hafta stay in this country, stay with us. But it’d be the worst mistake you ever made. You don’t belong here. You belong in school. You belong with your mamma. She needs you.”

Crutch was warming to the “Pappy-to-Son” talk.

“Another thing. You ain’t never seen this place in the winter. Hell, it ain’t even rained while you been here. When it snows and blizzards, you got to be out in it, pullin’ cows outa drifts, keepin’ baby calves from freezin’ to death, breakin’ ice so the cattle can drink, puttin’ out feed when snow covers the ground. There’s no end to it.

“And say you stick with cowboyin’ 10 years and are lucky and get to be foreman on some big fancy outfit like Don Webb’s. Top pay is $30. Whatcha gonna do if you wanna’ get married? Keep your wife and kids in the bunkhouse? Is that what you wanna’ do? What if you get hurt? Or she gets sick? You’re gonna’ be an old crippled-up man at 45 anyway, ranch life is so hard.

“Now, Son, take my advice and get outa here. I know you have differences with your mamma, but patch things up. You may think it’ll be tough, but I’ve seen you do things a lot tougher here. Go back home, take care of your mamma and the farm and finish school.”

By day's last light we forded the stream at the house and pulled up into the yard. We sat there a minute and Crutch said, "In three days Jack will be home from the rodeo. Roy asked me to bring you back as soon as Jack gets back, so that leaves you three days to chop up all that wood we got. That'll give you a chance to think."

I'd say Crutch and Maidie had a good supply of wood for the winter by the time I finished, with customized widths and lengths, too, and stacked according. I sure wished for a saw but made do with an ax. The cook stove took 6-inch lengths, split twice; the living room stove took 12-inch lengths, split once; the wash kettle outside took 18-inch lengths, not split; and then there was kindling, random lengths and split in slivers less than an inch.

There was lots of time to think. But I wasn't thinking about going home; that seemed to be settled. I was thinking how much I loved and would miss that country, doing cowboy stuff and being alone on my horse.

I read once, "You only have to be a cowboy once to define the rest of your life." It is the truth.

As Crutch had predicted, Jack rode in at the end of three days with pockets full of blue ribbons and prize money. He had done really well. Coincidentally, I'd just finished the wood chop-

ping, too, and we were feeling good that night. Maidie had breaded the salt pork with cornmeal before frying and even it tasted good.

About the salt pork. There was no refrigeration available and during the summer in remote areas like Crutch's, salt pork was about the only meat that would keep. Where Roy lived there was a cluster of ranches and one rancher would kill a yearling periodically and share it with the others, who had to consume all of it before it could go bad. In winter there was no problem with refrigeration; just put your beef in a gunny sack and hang it outside or in a tack room or someplace like that.

That night in the bunkhouse I asked Jack about rodeoing. He said I was already too tall for rodeo competition. Something about too much of my body sticking up above the saddle, which causes a higher center of gravity. Well, it was just a thought...

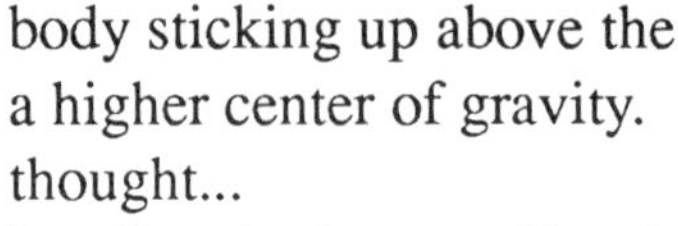

Next morning, I packed my stuff and Crutch drove me back to Roy's place, arriving about lunch time, and Crutch had a good time telling everyone about all my misadventures. Of course, by now it was funny, even to me, and we all had a good laugh. But he also told them I had been a good hand and was lots of help. I walked out to the car with him and shook hands. He looked me in the eyes and said, "Thanks for all you did, Son. I kinda wish you was my boy." He turned quickly and left.

Roy, Ora lee and the kids still were at the table. Ora Lee poured me another cup of coffee. There was some small talk and Roy said, "Kid, I got a letter from your

Mom. A neighbor is driving her here tomorrow to take you home. Did Crutch talk to you?"

I nodded that he had. "Did he tell you to come back if it doesn't work out?" I shook my head no, that he hadn't, because Crutch had not used those words. "Well, you can," Roy growled.

Then Roy said, "Kid, I want you to do something. Go down to the corral and saddle that horse you love so much and ride out and check all the windmills on this place. Winter's comin' on and I want to know that they're working good, the tanks are holding water all right and there's plenty of salt-lick around."

(Editor's notee: Salt lick is block salt which cattle like to lick. It seems essential to their well-being.)

Something seemed to be bothering Roy's eyes as he left the room. I never appreciated Roy more than at that moment. He knew I was brimming with emotion, how I felt about the horse, my new life and how badly I needed to be out alone in the saddle in that beautiful country, to sort things out and have the chance for a leisurely last look at everything that had come to mean so much to me.

My horse seemed to sense my mood and responded to patting on his neck and shoulders and rump. When I'd dismount he'd stay by my side and nudge my arm. I really loved that horse. I felt like we had a whole lot in common and that he recognized it, too.

When my mother and the neighbor arrived the next day, Ora Lee had seen to it that I was cleaned up and packed up. She had even trimmed my hair, which had gotten shaggy, and we'd borrowed Roy's straight razor and scraped the fuzz off my face.

She'd washed and pressed my shirt and pants, too, so I was ready to greet my mother looking pretty good.

When they arrived, it had been several years since everybody had seen one another, so it was howdying and hugging all around before we sat down to eat.

Another round of hugging and handshaking and we got in the car and left. Neither my mother or the neighbor said a word or asked a question about the runaway or what I'd been doing. It never came up, then or ever, although in later years she referred to that period as the time—as I mentioned early in this book—that she and I had "climbed fool's hill together."

EPILOGUE

When you got nothin' to lose, try anythin'

Another Runaway

After the continuing cowboy series had begun, several readers of The Godzilla Report owned up to running away from home when they were young tikes. When we were that young, going over the fence or out the gate on our own took a lot of courage, especially during depression and dust-bowl days.

As high-mileage adults now, we're not apt to talk much about those bad times of our youth, however humorous they seem now. Admitting that once upon a time we were that young, that poor, that foolish and that headstrong is hard.

Maybe "foolish" is the wrong word; what we did was accept and act upon what we thought was the only acceptable option we had, considering circumstances at the time. For those and many other reasons we deeply appreciate Leonard Pressley Ashton telling us this true story of his boyhood.

Pressley, as his relatives call him, is Wilsie's brother, (therefore, Skip's brother-in-law and the nephew of Skip's first wife, Vivian).

Skip, in his own tongue-in-cheek style, further described Pressley: "He has four daughters. Each time they tried they were hoping for a son. He says they would have tried again but heard that every fifth baby born is Chinese, so they stopped."

This is a story Pressley had never told before, even to his wife, LaVerne, his four daughters or his sister, Wilsie, who was a child when this all happened. That he wound up herding sheep makes this a truly amazing story, considering a fact well-known to his family and friends—a strong aversion to sheep and mutton.

For a little background, when Pressley was nine years old he and his mother, Elsie, his father, Doc, and his younger brother, Archie, were living in Electra, Texas. Wilsie hadn't arrived in this world yet. Everybody worked at whatever job they could get.

Pressley washed breakfast dishes at a cafe before going to school each morning, sold newspapers after school, and reported back to the cafe and washed dinner dishes that evening. At closing time, the cafe owner packaged up whatever cooked food was left over and gave it to Pressley to take home to his family, always including a pie.

Archie also sold papers and Doc did the few odd jobs he could find. Elsie, already in the early stages of tuberculosis although they didn't know it then, was too frail to do more than keep the house and family together. Pressley earned 50 cents a day at the cafe and about another 50 cents selling papers, and Archie also made another 50 cents selling papers. That was their only "steady" income.

By the time Pressley was 13 years old his family had rented his Grandmother Wilson's dry-land farm in Rolla Community, near Wellington, Texas, on an informal shares basis, and they were putting in crops. The ground had been plowed, and Doc asked Pressley to hook up a team to the section harrow, then harrow the ground to smooth it down and break up the clods.

(Editor's note: A section harrow was an early horse-drawn farm implement consisting of a rectangular steel framework mechanically attached to several rows of steel teeth underneath. The teeth were approximately 8 inches long, and their angle of attack to the ground was controllable by a single lever on top. They were called "section" harrows because you could hook two or more sections together, increasing the breadth of each pass, provided you had enough horses available, usually two per section. Generally, the operator walked behind the harrow, which created copious amounts of dust, or if it was a final pass and the teeth weren't set too deeply, some people laid a board across the framework and stood on the board while driving the horses. Skip is drawing from his own expertise. He used to have to operate a harrow, too.)

Like his mother, Pressley also had tuberculosis, but again,

no one was aware of it. (They were both diagnosed a year or so later and sent to a sanitarium for treatment and recuperation.) Walking and driving the horses in those terrible clouds of dust was causing all sorts of coughing and choking so bad Pressley felt he just couldn't take it, so he finally tied up the horses and went over to where Doc was working.

"Dad, he said, "The dust is so awful behind that harrow I just can't stand doing it any longer."

"Son," Doc replied, "You just have to do it. That's all there is to it."

Pressley coughed and wheezed his way through the rest of that day, while vowing to himself that he would never operate a harrow again in his lifetime. And, if that meant running away from home, so be it. Early the next morning, Pressley slipped some extra clothes into a cardboard box and quietly slipped away from home.

He had three $1 bills in his pocket.

He walked two miles north and four miles east to Highway 83, the highway to Abilene. He didn't know where he would go; he only knew that he had to get away.

Pressley caught a ride with a man who was going to San Angelo, Texas, which sounded like as good a destination as any, so he rode with him all the way. They drove all day, stopping once in Paducah. The man asked him if he had any money, and Pressley said, "Sure," and told him about the $3. The man bought their hamburgers for that meal.

It is assumed the man was joking when he asked Pressley later whether he was Democrat or Republican, but he grew very angry when Pressley answered, "Democrat." After all, his daddy was a Democrat, but the man lectured him severely on such political folly, then fell as silent as a tree full of owls in sunlight during the rest of the trip. Pressley decided it would be better not to tell anyone else who might ask.

They arrived in San Angelo about sundown. Pressley wandered around town awhile, hungry but not wanting to spend any of his money on food, and found a nice grassy place to sleep in a park. The next morning he approached some men nearby, who were talking and "spitting tobacco juice" and asked them about work.

They told him there was a man called "Chock" looking for someone to work on a sheep ranch and that he was due in town that morning. That sounded great to Pressley. He skipped breakfast, too, saving his $3.

About 9 or 10 that morning, Chock showed up and Pressley asked him about the job. He said he would pay $30 if Pressley stayed a month, and provide food and a bedroll. Pressley jumped on it. That sounded like paradise when men could hardly find jobs at all.

They left San Angelo and drove to the ranch, which was 40 miles southwest. Chock was from Brady and was grazing his sheep on ranch land belonging to a friend. He had a tent for provisions, 150 white sheep and a dog.

He cooked over a camp fire but the only things he cooked were hardtack bread, stewed mutton and coffee. Pressley learned his friend, Chock, was a Democrat and told him he was, too, and they got along really well together telling Republican jokes and talking politics. (For a 13-year-old? Knowing Pressley I can believe it.) The country was pretty, the work was pleasant and the weather good.

Everything was fine but that mutton stew. Pressley couldn't stomach the taste of it, the smell of it and after a short while, the thought of it. Mutton stew, three times a day. He thought he could survive on the hardtack, coffee and water but after awhile he began getting really hungry.

For 10 days they tended sheep by day, had mutton stew, hardtack and coffee, and slept on the ground in bedrolls. On the 10th day Pressley told Chock he was leaving. Chock said, "I sort of thought you would be," and gave Pressley 15 dollars, indicated he must have been really happy with Pressley's work. They shook hands.

Pressley walked several miles to the highway, but was

unable to get a ride and slept that night under a bridge. The next morning he caught a ride into San Angelo.

By now he was ravenously hungry and went to a cafe and bought six hamburgers for a quarter. He ate four there and took the other two with him for later.

His next ride was to Abilene and he was hungry again, having long since eaten his other two hamburgers. He asked the owner of a cafe if he could wash dishes in exchange for a meal.

The man said OK, so Pressley spent several hours washing dishes. The man fed him three hamburgers and a bottle of "red soda pop" and gave him a quarter.

It took five rides to get home: The one to Abilene, from Abilene to Anson, from Anson to Guthrie, from Guthrie to Paducach, from Paducah to Childress, and from Childress to where he began his trip, at the intersection of Highway 83.

From that point Pressley walked home. His greatest dread was what Doc would say or do to him. But when he got home, everyone... his Dad, Mom, Archie and baby Wilsie, acted as though he had never been gone. They didn't discuss the run-away with him; they didn't ask about his trip; they didn't punish him. But he was never again asked to run the harrow.

Pressley returned home with 18 dollars, the three he left with, which were still intact, plus the 15 he earned herding sheep. He gave that to his folks and it put food on the table for nearly a month.

#

EPILOGUE

Music won't cure the bite of a rattlesnake
But it's sure a soothin' universal language

About that Trumpet

Do you remember me mentioning that when I first ran away I carried all of my worldly possessions, including a trumpet, in a trumpet case? You may have noticed I never mentioned that trumpet again.

Well, one reason is that I never got to use it on my travels. Not once! Before leaving home I was banging the trumpet, trombone and saxophone for school and church affairs and when some of us who were so inclined would get together just for fun.

Bobbie Lee is and was an accomplished pianist and before she left home for college and teaching we had long jam sessions after work in the evenings. I took the trumpet when I ran away, thinking I might be reduced to playing it on a street corner or something, or just to have something to toot on if I got lonely. The other reason I took it was because it was a lot lighter weight and less bulky than either the sax or trombone, and there was just enough room to pack my pennies and other worldly goods inside the case around the trumpet.

You know, those crazy New Mexico cow people kept me so busy I never even took the trumpet out of its case. I'm sure they didn't even know I had a trumpet. But I suppose if I didn't bow or pick a stringed musical instrument they wouldn't have understood, anyway.

As an aside, it might interest you to know that during my senior year in Kosciusko, Mississippi, I played bass horn in the high school and Development Association bands, and played a hot saxophone every Saturday night in a little local dance band. That old sax largely paid my way through school that year, and it was a borrowed sax at that.

Well, that old trumpet is long gone, and so is that saxophone. But I have another saxophone now, and this is one of those strange "It's a small world" episodes. It's about one of those ghosts from your past that mysteriously intertwines into the lives of many of your friends whose paths have crossed yours through the years.

Before the editor had met and swept his beautiful wife, Jo, off her feet she was dating one of her high school friends, a nice kid named John Hornback. He had an old "C Melody" sax he wanted to trade to me for a small radio to take along when he went away to college. Now, 50 years later, I still have that old sax. Haven't played it, but I get it out every 10 years or so and look at it. Kinda reminds me of that neat little girl named Jo.

Howdy, Y'All

(In typical Panhandle friendliness, Skip has offered an invitation to his readers: "If you're ever back this way we'd sure like you to drop in for a cup of coffee.")

#

OTHER ITEMS BY OUR CARTOONIST, A.W. ERWIN

Books
No. 1 Jus' Horsin'-Round
No. 2 Round-Em Up
No. 3 Tales from the Outhouse
No. 4 More Horsepower!
Plus more currently in progress

Calendars - Greeting Cards
Coffee Mugs - T-shirts
And More!
(DEALER INQUIRIES WELCOME)

Cartoons available for Newspapers,
Magazines & Newsletters, etc.

Custom Artwork & Logos

For more information on
A.W. ERWIN & his
HOOVES & HORNS COWTOONS

WRITE TO:
HOOVES & HORNS COWTOONS
P.O. BOX 591
GRAHAM, TX 76046

Hey, Buckaroo, didja enjoy this li'l ol' book? Do you know some fellow wranglers who'd enjoy some tall but true cowboy stories about how the West really was? From a lanky, tall-in-the-saddle, cow pie and cactus cowboy who's been there, done it all and who tells it with homespun, rib-tickling humor?

Well, pardner, y'all just tear out this here page, fill out the order form and we can ship to you pronto, or directly to the gift recipient with a card saying this is the gol-darndest gift from an old saddle tramp like you.

To order by mail, y'all just fill out the order form below and mail to: Skip-Don Publications, 117 White Chapel Drive, Benicia, CA 9451 or 6420 Euston Drive, Amarillo, TX 79109. For information, send inquiries by fax to (806) 354-0602, or by e-mail to keller6325@aol.com or cactus@netjava.com

Please add shipping & handling charge of $3 for first book, $1.50 for each additional book in same order. California buyers add 7.25% to cover price, Texas buyers add 8.25% (per book).

______copies at $9.95 each = Subtotal____________________

Tax____________________

Shipping ____________________

Total____________________

Ship to:

Name______________________Address____________________________

City/State/Zip____

Phone (____)_____________________(In case of questions about your order)

Note—We'll mail your extra copies directly to the recipient if you prefer, and we'll even slip in a gift card saying it's from you. Add names and addresses below:

Name______________________Address____________________________

City/State/Zip____

Name______________________Address____________________________

City/State/Zip____

$$$ See next page for bulk rate discounts. $$$

Buy 20 or more and save!

If your order adds up to 20 or more, you qualify for the bulk rate of $5.95 per book. You also save on shipping and handling. Fill out form and send with check to: Skip-Don Publications at 117 White Chapel Drive, Benicia, CA 94510, or 6420 Euston Drive, Amarillo, TX 79109.

Ask about discounts for orders of 100 or more

- *For bulk orders of 20 or more, shipping is 45 cents per book.*
- *For orders of 19 or less, shipping is $3 per book for the first book, $1.50 per book in same order thereafter.*
- *California buyers add 7.25% sales tax to book price.*
- *Texas buyers add 8.25% sales tax to book price.*

Amount of order $____________________ paid by check or money order.

Name____

Company____

Address____

City________________________ State______ Zip____________

Phone: (________)________________ Fax: (______)______________

e-mail____